PRA
WRITE YOUR _
By Douglas Winslow Cooper, Ph.D.

"If you're thinking about writing your own book and need inspiration, step-by-step guidance and lots of encouragement, this book is for you. Doug Cooper writes in an approachable style, and his scientific background comes through as he analyzes and picks apart the actions you need to take to make your book a success. From getting into the right frame of mind, to planning, writing, publishing and marketing (or as Doug says 'payoffs = plan x prepare x publish x promote'), this book contains all you need to make your own a success."

Ginny Carter, The Author Maker,
www.marketingtwentyone.co.uk

✦✦✦✦

"I wish I had a copy of *Write Your Book with Me* as I wrote my first book in 1994. The process by which you can write a book is spelled out step by step, with time-lines, accountability tables, and all the resources necessary to make the journey a pleasure. If you ever thought writing a book was impossible, I encourage you to pick up this book, and you'll see the possibilities."

Edison Guzman, President,
A&E Advertising and Web Design

✦✦✦✦

"Dr. Cooper's academic credentials (Ph.D. from Harvard, etc.) led me to expect academic writing—technical and boring. I discovered, to my delight, that I was completely wrong. In these pages I found a great intellect reading widely in the field, consolidating the most practical tips, and expressing them in crisp, down-to-earth prose. He's also honest—neither promising nor claiming best-selling status—but telling us candidly what works (and doesn't work) for him and others, motivating us by his passion for writing and his genuine concern for helping fellow writers along the way. In the rapidly changing writing and publishing industry, I needed a refresher and update before publishing my latest book. This one more than met my need!"

J. Steve Miller, author of *Sell More Books!* and *Why Brilliant People Believe Nonsense: A Practical Text on Critical and Creative Thinking*

ﭰﭰﭰ

"As a budding novelist, I've read a lot of books on how to write. A lot. I wish I'd had access to this book sooner. Ever the scientist, Dr. Cooper has extensively researched what the experts (Stephen King, Dan Poynter, and others) have said, and then distilled it into a comprehensive text. He covers all the different formats: fiction, non-fiction, and memoir.

"The book starts with an excellent section on why to write in the first place, then covers preparation, the actual act of writing, publishing, promoting and marketing. It covers the whole *enchilada*. The best part, in my opinion, is how the author illuminates each section with examples from his own memoir, *Ting and I*.

"If you're contemplating writing and publishing, this book should be in your inventory."

Dr. G.E. Nolly, author of the *Hamfist* series

PRAISE FOR
TING AND I:
A MEMOIR OF LOVE, COURAGE, AND DEVOTION
by Douglas Winslow Cooper

"This book reads like the book *Love Story,* but with the harsh realities of how a couple deals with a catastrophic illness....***Ting and I* is a must-read for any health care professional."** Patricia A. Burns, Ph.D., R.N., Professor of Nursing.

"Whether it be close friendships, lifetime companions or marriage soul-mates, this book clearly illustrates what it means to be a human being." **Amazon reviewer (5 stars).**

"This is a poignant saga of a brilliant, beautiful young Chinese woman who fell in love with an American Ivy League student that tugs at the heartstrings." **Amazon reviewer (5 stars).**

"It is unique because the people it is about are unique. God bless them both." **Amazon reviewer (5 stars).**

"The memoir was a great read!" **Amazon reviewer (4 stars).**

"Poignant story of true love and commitment." **Amazon reviewer (5 stars).**

WRITE
Your Book
WITH ME

Payoffs = Plan x Prepare x Publish x Promote

Douglas Winslow Cooper, Ph.D.

outskirtspress
DENVER, COLORADO

DEDICATION

To Tina Su Cooper,
my beloved wife and continuing inspiration,
and to our dear sons,
Philip Y. Chiang and Theodore Y. Chiang.

STEPHEN KING'S FOREWORD TO HIS
ON WRITING

This is a short book because most books about writing are filled with bullshit. Fiction writers, present company [King] included, don't understand very much about what they do—not why it works when it's good, not why it doesn't when it's bad. I figured the shorter the book, the less the bullshit.

One notable exception to the bullshit rule is The Elements of Style, *by William Strunk, Jr. and E.B. White. There is little or no detectable bullshit in that book. (Of course it's short; at eighty-five pages it's much shorter than this one.) I'll tell you right now that every aspiring writer should read* The Elements of Style. *Rule 17 in the chapter titled Principles of Composition is, "Omit needless words." I will do that here.*

[This is King's Second Foreword to his *On Writing: A Memoir of the Craft.*]

ACKNOWLEDGMENTS

Cheryl C. Cohen, Director of Membership Investment at the Orange County [N.Y.] Chamber of Commerce, has once again aided me with her skilled edtorial assistance.

Edison Guzman, President of A&E Advertising and Web Design [aeadvertising.com], has warmly encouraged and expertly advised me.

PREFACE

You know you want to write a book, and I know I can help you. My book will help you get started, and my coaching enterprise [writeyourbookwithme.com] is available to give you personalized help, like a personal trainer does for those who want to get fit.

I just Googled "how to write a book," and I found 25 million entries...lots of interest, lots of advice. I've added to that collection. Information comes nearly free, consultation and coaching do not. Since you are here now, "love the one you're with," and let me help you write, publish, and promote your book to get you to your payoff, whatever that may be.

You can do well by doing good, as author and entrepreneur Jorge S. Olson (2009) writes:

Want to be famous? Start writing.

Writing is one of the greatest and most noble ways of unselfish self-promotion. Through your writing you are able to entertain, you can teach, and you allow your readers to imagine and dream. Writing is truly one of the ultimate tools for unselfish self-promotion.

The Internet site **writeyourbookwithme.com** describes the coaching business I established after writing and publishing my own *Ting and I: A Memoir of Love, Courage, and Devotion.* What I did I can teach you to do. I don't guarantee you a bestseller or financial success, but if you follow the path I've taken, you will have written and published your book, promoted it to let others know it exists, and perhaps even profited financially from the process.

payoffs = plan x prepare x publish x promote

This sub-title of mine implies that **each step builds on the preceding ones.** You will gain from having planned and then prepared your text, gain more by publishing and then promoting it, and you may even profit from it directly or indirectly, getting a payoff that you sought. If the equation were exact and if you improved each of the factors on the right-hand side by 20%, your payoff would more than double. A retired physicist, I love equations, even ones that need a bit of interpretation.

Certainly, you will gain a sense of pride in your accomplishment, like completing a marathon. Those who read your book will gain from the experience.

Jump right in. The water is fine. I hope you will be entertained, energized, and educated by what you read here.

Douglas Winslow Cooper, Ph.D.
douglas@tingandi.com
http://writeyourbookwithme.com
http://managenursingcareathome.com
http://douglaswinslowcooper.blogspot.com
http://twitter.com/douglaswcooper
https://www.facebook.com/tingandi
phone: 845.778.4204
264 East Drive
Walden, NY 12586-2329

GREETINGS: GETTING STARTED

Today, Sunday, I'm getting serious about writing this book for you. The day you start to read this may be the day you, too, get started seriously on your own book.

Pretty early in the process, you should set up a method to keep track of your progress. In management, they often say "if it isn't measured, it isn't managed." So, by keeping track of your progress in terms of word count, you can see how well you're doing, congratulate yourself when you're doing well, scold yourself when you are a bit behind schedule. You'll find that just the little reward of self-praise and the little punishment of self-blame will accelerate your progress. Incentives incent.

For me, I started by outlining this book a week or two ago, but now I'm beginning to write. My **progress record will be: the day, what I worked on, the cumulative word count, and the added amount**. Here's my first week:

WEEK ONE	Final Word Count	Change
Saturday, outlined.	w/c= 500.	Added 500.
Sunday, wrote up to WHY WRITE.	w/c= 2,500.	Added 2,000.
Sunday, added prior blogs.	w/c=17,900.	Added 15,400.
Sunday, more writing.	w/c=20,100.	Added 2,200.
Monday, more writing.	w/c=21,840.	Added 1,740.
Tuesday, more writing.	w/c=24,800.	Added 2,960
Tuesday, deleted 1000 duplicates.	w/c=23,870.	Added - 930
Wednesday, organized, planned, wrote.	w/c=26,030.	Added 2,160.

WEEK ONE	Final Word Count	Change
Thursday, wrote.	w/c=26,880.	Added 850.
Friday, wrote nothing, added file.	w/c= 27,350.	Added 470.

You get the idea. I've put my whole progress and effort record in Appendix I. Bestselling author Shelley Hitz (2015) recommends an even more detailed tracking of your progress, including calculating words per minute written. Well, "whatever floats your boat," as they say, whoever "they" are.

A good feature of Microsoft's Word is that it displays unobtrusively your page count, page position, and word count. Another nice feather is "autocorrect," which caught and changed my initial misspelling of "unobtrusively." Sadly, it sometimes guesses wrong, so you can get "fort" instead of "font." Beware.

I got a head start by having material I had already written for my blog, and I am a fast writer, so there are days when I added 1000 words in a few hours. Your speed will vary, but aim for a pace you find you can usually achieve. **Try to write every day. As noted above, keep track of your effort or your output or both,** so you see how well you are doing. Accomplishment feels good. Slacking off, not so much. The day I didn't write, I felt I should have. Life intruded.

WHY WRITE YOUR BOOK? WHY NOT BLOG?

The late, highly esteemed educator and management expert Stephen R. Covey (1989) advised in his classic book *The Seven Habits of Highly Effective People*, that we **"begin with the end in mind." Let us turn our attention to that. Why are you writing a book? What do you hope to get by doing so?**

Recently, discussing this project with my thirty-something younger son, Phil, and his long-time girlfriend, Lisa, the question was raised: **why write a book instead of a blog?** Is it just a generational thing?

A blog has the advantage that you can present it in bits and pieces over a prolonged period of time, and you can get feedback from others as the project goes along.

A book frequently has a long gestation before it is born, though it doesn't have to. Writing a book is a somewhat lonely task, where with few exceptions you are not getting input from other people as you go along.

A book seems to have more prominence and permanence than a blog, however. There is a sense of accomplishment, along with a certain amount of esteem given to the author, a feeling of having written something that will endure that a blog rarely provides. **Authors are authorities. Memoirs mold memories.** Completing the "memoir marathon" doesn't quite make you rare, but certainly makes you stand out.

In fact, the lines are blurring between blog and book. I blogged my memoir after I wrote it. I'll use pieces of my blog [douglas-winslowcooper.blogspot.com] in this book. Many other writers have done likewise.

REASONS TO WRITE A BOOK

In the professions, **being the author of a book generally trumps merely having written some articles.** Lenny Golino, currently a private investigator and formerly a NYPD homicide detective, with whom I co-authored his memoir, *The Shield of Gold*, referred to the book as a "thick business card," and he reports that it indeed got him P.I. jobs he would not have been likely to get otherwise. Writing his book he found to be somewhat cathartic, and he also gets a sense of satisfaction when he gives the book to potential clients.

Getting something off your chest, getting relief from feelings you have suppressed, telling the world how things should be... all are good reasons to write and publish your book.

Writing can be therapeutic. In her very well received book, *Writing Can Get You through the Tough Times: No Experience Necessary*, author and writing coach M.J. Hanley-Goff (2014) extols the value of journal-writing as a form of psychological self-help that can bring insights to the writers and their readers. She tells how writing regularly helped her through panic attacks that were nearly debilitating, spurring her to solicit, collect, and publish the writings of others around the country who used keeping a journal to help them overcome the damage from child abuse, the upheavals from divorce and abandonment or loss of a loved one, the fears accompanying diagnoses of crippling or life-threatening illnesses, the emotional time bombs of battlefield PTSD, and similar drastic life challenges.

Many of those featured in this collection went on to publish their reflections, either as they were or in fictional form, bringing what they learned to others who could benefit. She quotes the Association for Psychological Science: **"merely putting pen to paper to express one's emotional ailments has benefits for mental and physical health."** The writers I have worked with have often told me this was true for them.

Rob Hillman (2015) in his ebook *17 Reasons Why YOU Should Write a Book* included:

- The time is ripe. You will not live forever. The internet makes it easy to gather material and publish it.
- People need to know what you know. Each life is unique.
- Publishing gives you and your ideas leverage.
- Change fear of doing it to fear of failing to do it.
- "Leave your footprints in the sand." Let 'em know you were here.
- Gain credibility and authority, as an author. Impress your friends. Confound your enemies.
- Write for charity, if not for yourself. Donate your earnings.
- Change the world…a little, at least.
- It is easier than you think.
- Do it for someone else. My memoir was mostly for my wife.
- Enhance your resume.
- Get revenge. Be careful with this. Change the names to protect the guilty.
- Gain personal satisfaction. You are an author! You did it.

I'll let Stephen King (in his *On Writing*) have the penultimate statement about the goal:

Writing isn't about making money, getting famous, getting dates, getting laid, or making friends. In the end, it's about enriching the lives of those who will read your work, and enriching your own life, as well.

Finally, some people just love books. Comedian Groucho Marx said, "Outside of a dog, a book is man's best friend. Inside of a dog, it's too dark to read."

TABLE OF CONTENTS

CHAPTER 1

PLAN

*If you don't know where you are going,
you'll end up someplace else.*
Yogi Berra

When taking a trip, you need a destination, a goal.

Next, you need a road map. Without a plan, you are lost.

I hope this book will serve you as kind of a map, one based on the advice of many wise writers and on my own experience, as I have already helped about a half-dozen would-be authors write and publish their first books. The pre-eminent mathematician/physicist Isaac Newton modestly asserted that he had seen farther because he had "stood on the shoulders of giants." The many sources cited here have, at least, given me piggyback rides.

WHAT KIND OF BOOK?

What kind of book do you want to write? Sometimes, the answer is obvious. In fact, you might want to wait until it is self-evident.

My co-author Mary E. Seaman wrote her memoir, *Kidnapped Twice: Then Betrayed and Abused,* to tell her story of having been abused as a child, as an object lesson to others about the terrible repercussions of such treatment on those who are defenseless. While Mary perhaps could have made the book into a novel, into fiction, and thus hid completely the names and places involved, she chose to try to tell the truth, and by labeling it as nonfiction to have it make a greater impact on its readers. Naming the good people lets us reward them. Naming the bad should shame those who have treated us poorly…though one does so judiciously, as they have little recourse other than a lawsuit.

Another of the writers that I have worked with, **Loretta Quisenberry Pickens, chose to write a historical novel, *The Last Drumbeat,* based on the true experiences of her ancestors,** made more interesting by being put into the form of a novel, where conversations that cannot be known can be imagined and presented. Telling the story by relying solely on facts that could be corroborated would likely have produced a book much less interesting and compelling. L.Q. has written the book partly to give the perspective of Southerners who were not slave-owners, yet who supported the South during our Civil War.

A third writer of mine, Adria Goldman Gross, has co-authored with me a book, *SOLVED! Curing Your Medical Insurance Problems,* telling how to assure that the medical bills that one receives are correct and how to be sure that insurance companies are reimbursing you as they should, all based on her experience as a patient's advocate for these matters. The book is a mix of thick business card, how-to handbook, and implied critique of some of the practices by medical providers and insurers in America today.

Two other writers whose books I edited—Alice Conner Selfridge (2014), *High Shoes and Bloomers,* and Kathleen Blake Shields (2015), *Home is Where the Story Begins*—**produced memoirs of happy childhoods, rather rare in the memoir genre,** giving us uplifting tales of growing up in happy families despite near-poverty.

Sometimes the book you write will have unexpected consequences. I credit my memoir, *Ting and I,* with helping to persuade my former employer, three years after I published it, to continue to spend hundreds of thousands of dollars yearly on my beloved wife Tina's skilled nursing care at home. A co-author of mine, Marie Elizabeth Foglia, wrote a book describing why she had reason to believe that she was the unacknowledged daughter of the movie star Ava Gardner. That book (Cooper & Foglia, 2012) led to a DNA test with an Ava Gardner relative, the results of which indicated that Marie was mistaken in this belief. While it was not the outcome she expected or wanted, it did produce an answer.

Two of "my writers" had political motives for writing. Judy Axtell's memoir, *But...at What Cost,* tells her life story, as a progression from being a liberal in a multi-generational and multi-racial extended family to joining the conservative Tea Party movement. Shaun Adkins is writing *Squashing Liberalism,* a political polemic that may propel him to political office and already has helped garner him an Internet talk-show.

Why write a book? It's the long-form version. A Tweet is 140 characters or less. Your epitaph will hardly be much longer. Who knows how big your blog will be and how long your blog will last? You write for yourself, the way you might work out at a gym or prepare for and run a marathon, and you write for others, to inform, persuade, entertain, thank, criticize….

WRITE FOR YOURSELF? GET SATISFACTION, REGARDLESS OF SALES

When you finish something difficult, like running a long-distance race, building a boat or a set of bookshelves, painting a room or drawing a portrait, **you have done something worthwhile primarily for yourself.** There's at least an element of that in every finished and published book.

Authors would love to have bestsellers, but satisfaction can come even from giving away as many as you sell, the case for my memoir and true for most memoirs by non-famous folks.

Ideally, you'll have a passion about your topic. The book-writing challenge takes, at the least, a strong desire. You will need to be more passionate about it than I was when being recruited for Officer Candidate School [OCS] while in the Army. From my memoir:

When the Army called, so to speak, I was in fine shape. Basic training (Ft. Gordon, GA) was not too tough. As noted above, I had played, enthusiastically but not very skillfully, several sports in high school, continued basketball in intramurals at Cornell, and had boxed a bit my freshman year. I liked to think of myself as fairly tough. Not tough enough to be a Ranger or a Marine, but tough enough for the Army, as my basic-training experience confirmed.

I was, however, a mediocre marksman with the rifle, though not on purpose. It did not seem I was Infantry material, although I admired the toughness of those who were.

Testing put my I.Q. near [redacted], and I was part of a small group of recruits they called together to try to induce us to become officers. It would mean extending my two-year draft commitment to three years. The closing line in the recruitment film was, "Don't go to Officer Candidate School unless these gold bars mean more to you than anything else." That convinced me: two years and out.

Commitment! To finish a book, you need to be more than merely involved; you need to be committed. The difference? In a ham-and-egg sandwich, the chicken is involved, but the pig is committed.

Granted, the writing process may increase your enthusiasm, with the prospect of a published book. **Progress encourages. Success breeds success.** Even if the topic is not one you are excited about, smart people adapt. To quote again from my classic memoir:

My mother is a brilliant woman. Did I mention that she went through U. Mass., Amherst, in three years, rather than four, and that she graduated near the top of her class? An English major, she did some journalism work after the family nest was empty. Before that, though, during a slow period when the family lived in Rosendale, N.Y., she thought it would be fun to join MENSA and see whom we'd meet.

MENSA is an organization for people in the top 2 percent of intelligence, as measured by an IQ test. She took the test, sur-

passed the requirement easily, and signed up. Somewhat later, she held a little get-together for other MENSA folk in the area. I think we had a half-dozen at our house. All were undoubtedly bright. Except for my mother, they seemed to rank low on the social-skills-quotient [SSQ?] scale. Some were obvious misfits. We got to know one whom we would see occasionally wandering loose from his group home in Kingston, NY.

A memorable moment occurred when one MENSA guest described how she handled a job interview at a company that specialized in construction materials. She told them, "I love cement."

If it is, of necessity, the topic of your book, you too may need to come to love cement.

WRITE FOR AN AUDIENCE? INVESTIGATE WHAT SELLS

If writing primarily to reach a large audience, check out which books are bestsellers, using amazon.com, where a wealth of valuable information is readily available. As you do that, you will see that there are many, many categories of book types— genres. Balance your personal interests with some cunning to seek a genre or topic that is both popular and yet not too crowded. That will take some skill.

Look at what is popular at: ezinearticles.com, amazon.com, dummies.com, magazines.com, udemy.com.

Chandler Bolt (2015), in his *Book Launch*, gives helpful details on choosing a topic that will likely sell, listing the following how-to **book topics as particularly popular:**

1. Diet and fitness
2. Relationships or breakups
3. Time management, stress management
4. How to make more money

Among the books of the type that you hope to write, look at reviews of the most popular of these, and see what the favorable reviewers had to say as well as what a few of the unfavorable reviewers criticized, to help guide you in determining what you need to imitate, and what's missing that you can supply.

While there is something to be said for being so creative as to come up with something entirely new, this is extremely rare. Recall the adage, "There is nothing new under the sun."

In marketing, those sellers who hope to enter the marketplace are advised to copy what is successful, then change it a bit to make it better, "the same, but different." Writers should heed this as well. You know that you like certain types of books and movies, and outside of that sphere, you are not likely to be a customer.

It is said, harkening back to the days of the old West, that the **pioneers got the arrows, while the settlers got the cash.** Unless you have a particularly good new idea, you probably want to be a settler rather than a pioneer.

WHO IS YOUR AUDIENCE? DEMOGRAPHICS: AGE, SEX, LOCATION, RACE, INCOME, POLITICS, ETHNICITY, MARITAL STATUS...

Although we would like to write a book that appeals to almost all readers, we cannot.

Age makes some material inappropriate or unfathomable for some readers.

Men and women generally have rather different tastes.

Certain races and ethnicities will be more drawn to books about people like themselves than about outsiders.

"The rich are not like us," it has been said, and this extends to tastes in reading matter, to a degree. Class differences count.

We know that politics, liberal versus conservative, Democrat versus Republican, has opened a Great Divide in public opinion, and this extends to the books the partisans prefer.

Unmarried women tend to have different preferences than do married women, *etc*. Married men differ from unmarried men in book preferences, too.

It is probably best to try to imagine your ideal reader, and please that person, while avoiding things that are very likely to alienate your non-ideal readers. Sometimes, however, there are hard truths that you want to convey, welcome or not. Just know that you pay a price in reduced popularity and acceptance by doing so.

OUTLINE NEEDED

You'll need an outline. Write down a half-dozen or so basics, then do some free-association thinking, some brainstorming.

I'll discuss later a variety of book types, but one popular form is the memoir. If you are going to write a memoir, the story of part of your life, as you experienced it, it will be not the whole truth, but some of it, and none of it should be false, although nobody's memory is perfect. You start with a simple outline and then fill in the details.

Here is a very simple preliminary outline for your memoir:

- **Crisis:** catch the reader's attention with something dramatic.
- **Background:** what led up to it.
- **Outcome:** what followed, immediately and in the long run.
- **Lessons learned**: what did you learn and what can others take away?

Let's analyze my own memoir with respect to this outline:

- **Crisis:** In the first book that I wrote, *Ting and I: a Memoir of Love, Courage, and Devotion,* the first chapter describes the life-and-death situation my wife, Tina (born "Su Ting-ting" in China), faced due to an exacerbation of her multiple sclerosis that left her quadriplegic, on a ventilator, fed and medicated through a gastric tube, with the prognosis that she would live only a few months.
- **Background:** Who are these people? How did they come to this point in their lives? What is the cause of the crisis? What is the possible resolution? How likely is that? The next chapters traced Tina's life and mine to our meeting, our parting, our re-uniting, and our marriage. Then her multiple sclerosis worsened.
- **Outcome**: What followed from the crisis? What are the

implications both for the writer and for people who he/ she really cares about? Tina's life as a quadriplegic and mine as a caregiver and care-manager were described.

- **Lessons learned:** What did the writer take away from this
- experience? What should others learn as well? My themes were the power of love, the importance of marriage, the value of life even when seriously disabled.

That was pretty easy, wasn't it?

Because memoirs are stories, we can profit from the advice of S. Evans (2015) with respect to novels, **start with a bang:** "The beginning of the story is what is going to capture the reader…." He says to **make them wonder about the outcome of something.** Sketch the setting, the way a cartoonist would. Introduce the main character, someone to like or dislike strongly. Give only a little background information.

The memoir will have lots of stories. As with fiction, the writer needs to make sure the reader learns the answers to the questions journalists pose for themselves: **Who? What? When? Where? Why? How?** The little stories need to **start with implicit headlines** to alert the reader to what is coming: "It was a dark and stormy night…." Snoopy knew what to write! [Though Edward Bullwer-Lytton's opening line has often been mocked.]

Another popular type is the how-to book. Let's develop a short outline format:

- **What you are trying to do.**
- **Why it is important to you.**
- **Materials you'll need.**

- Step-by-step instructions for accomplishing it.
- What the outcome should be.
- Sources of information and materials.

Again, the outline is straightforward. We'll discuss this kind of book in more detail below, too.

For this book of mine, *WYBWM*, I had an outline of approximately 30 chapters. I put the outline at the beginning of my manuscript, and then I copied it again and added it below the first one. That's where I planned to write the details under the various headings of the outline.

As I went along, I checked off in the first outline the sections that I completed. If I added new sections, I put them both in the initial outline and in the outline that forms the framework for the body of the book. I recommend you do this also. Hopefully, this keeps you on track.

With an outline, you are already getting a good idea of what you're going to need to finish writing the book. If it is a memoir, look at letters, memorabilia, programs, publications of yours, photo albums, and records of a vast variety of types. If it's a how-to book, you'll want to be gathering written materials and videos other people have used to try to explain what it is that you will be explaining.

Since *WYBWM* is essentially a how-to book, I have indeed spent some time gathering materials prepared by myself and others to help guide and support its writing.

Recently, Britain's Ginny Carter, "The Author Maker," wrote a

fine book on outlining as the key to writing your book. I wrote the following highly enthusiastic review of it for amazon.com:

THE BUSINESS BOOK OUTLINE BUILDER

Ginny Carter refers to herself as The Author Maker, and she does in Britain many of the same things I do in America: we help others to write and publish their books. She and I have corresponded occasionally, and she is a pleasure to know. When I saw her book I was inclined to like it, and my expectations were upheld.

As it is a book about outlining a book, the crucial step in building a framework on which the whole edifice depends, I'll adopt her own outline to tell you about the book…which you should get if you are planning to write a non-fiction book relating to a business you have or wish to have.

Introduction

Ms. Carter starts with a bang, as you should, "When we open a business book it's a bit like stepping into the author's imaginary home; each room holds a different aspect of their thinking and knowledge." She's personal, direct, interesting, and conversational.

We are reassured we will not be wasting our time in reading this concise guide: "In this guide, I use the exact same techniques I use with my clients. So I know they work, and they will for you too."

Taking her own advice, offered later in the book, she quickly offers a helpful download in return for our precious email address.

Then she gets right to it:

Step 1: What Do You Want Your Book to Achieve?

"It sounds like a funny question, doesn't it? You've probably been dreaming of writing a book for quite a while, so asking *why* you want one seems beside the point." But this is exactly on point.

Your goals in writing the book will shape everything that follows, so they need careful attention. You can't get There if you don't know where There is. Your goals will shape your writing and your book promotion. A "business book," as she defines it here, is a book that furthers a business you have or hope to have. Most "businesses" make money, but some are charitable or even hobbies that enrich the lives of their "proprietors."

A well-done book will add to your *gravitas*, your credibility, your client or email list, and your sense of satisfaction. Stephen King once noted [in his memoir, *On Writing*] that it will not likely help you get dates, but that is another issue.

Step 2: Who Do You Want to Read Your Book?

You might answer "everyone." More modestly, you might want friends and family to be sure to marvel at and mull over your *magnum opus,* but a "business" book has as its targets prospective customers and those who influence people to become customers. If you are a writer, you are looking for gigs. A coach wants those who would want to be coached. Medical and legal professionals, for example, seek to raise their stature (and their incomes) by being authors, authorities…while giving the readers something of value instead of self-aggrandizement, which does not sit well with most who read books.

You have to target your audience, often the more specifically the better, as those who know you are talking about them will resonate to your message the way others will not. Targeting often involves an awareness of demographics, as well as a knowledge of needs and interests.

Step 3: What's Your Book About?

"Your book needs to have a BIG MESSAGE. And that message should be the answer to a single, burning problem or question—the very one your readers are grappling with right now."

Here's her formula that can work well for most of these books:

"I want to help _____ (your target readers) to _____ (your big message) so I can _____ (your goal)."

If this review were a book, my example would be: I want to help <u>aspiring non-fiction authors</u> to <u>decide to buy this book</u> so <u>they and their writing coach will prosper</u>.

That was easy.

Step 4: Let's Outline Your Book!

Ms. Carter gives several detailed examples of outlines that can work well. She has selected five types of "business" book:

1. Transformational memoir (your story and how your readers can learn from it)
2. Coaching programme into a book (the method by which you help your clients make a transformation)
3. Inspirational book
4. Self-help guide
5. Collection of interviews

Step 5: How to Market Your Business in Your Book

You'll want to trade some additional material of value for email addresses, and a wise businessperson will include snippets about the business within the text. See her book for additional comments.

End Note

There's lots more in this book that a review cannot cover, and I invite readers who hope to become authors to get this book.

About the Author

I'll let her book tell you: *"....So after some soul searching she gathered the courage to follow her dreams and put this talent, together with her lifelong writing skills, to more powerful use as a business book ghostwriter and book writing coach."*

꣠꣠꣠

HOW TO WRITE IT?

It was said half-jokingly by the late sportswriter Red Smith, **"Writing is easy: you just open a vein and bleed."** Hopefully, you'll have an easier time.

My authors-to-be have given me their work in various forms: handwritten, typed, in computer files, and even over the phone as I interviewed them, later to be dictated by me into a computer file using Dragon Naturally Speaking speech-to-text transcription.

"How to write it?" means, in part, how to come up with the ideas needed and how to keep going when initial enthusiasm wanes?

Chandler Bolt in his *Book Launch* advises the writer to:

- **Fail first, then learn.** Take action. Tweak your rough draft.
- **Be accountable to someone.** Make and keep a commitment.
- **Take consistent action.** Develop a "system" for your efforts.
- **Write a contract with yourself.**
- **Remind yourself why you are writing a book:** reputation, money and leads for business, growing your network, pushing your passion project...even saving the world or the community.

Bolt swears by the following simple system for generating the content and writing your book:

- Mind-map. Put your subject at the center and then dream up topics that connect to it, like a spider web.
- From the mind-map entries, develop an outline.
- From the outline, write a first draft, without correcting it significantly until you have reached the end, and give yourself a due date for reaching that end

- For each chapter, put yourself on the clock. For example, mini-mind-map for 12 minutes, outline for 12 minutes, write for 90 minutes.
- Eliminate distractions. Turn them all off.
- Write in the morning, first thing.
- Establish a writing pattern: time and place, consistently.
- Remember that "done is better than perfect," or as the French say [in French, naturally], "the best is the enemy of the good." Your book will never be perfect, and your readers do not expect perfection.
- Get help with editing: content editing to make sure the subject is covered well, copy editing to make sure there are few if any spelling or grammatical errors, etc.

I started writing my memoir by listing on the left-hand side of the page each year from my birth year, 1942, to the then-current year, 2011. I made notes about things that happened to me, and sometimes in the world at large, by each year. Faint memories became sharper, as one thing suggested another. Leave more room than you expect to need. Scrapbooks helped, too. Overnight, I kept a pad and pen by my bedside and would jot notes down as memories surfaced. Googling places and historic events brought them back more forcefully. These tactics worked.

As the Nike sportswear ads urge, **"just do it." Put pen to paper, fingers to keyboard, or even dictate it**…as I am doing for much of this book. "If you build it, they will come;" ideas, that is… readers will need some cajoling. **If you sit down and either do nothing or write something, you'll write.** To become more effective, develop Stephen Covey's 7 habits, described next.

APPLYING COVEY'S *7 HABITS OF HIGHLY EFFECTIVE PEOPLE*

Twenty-six years ago, the late Stephen R. Covey rocked the personal-growth and keys-to-success world with his book *The 7 Habits of Highly Effective People,* a bestseller that made him famous.

Before detailing the 7 habits, Covey (1989, 2010) distinguished his approach from that of so many of his predecessors in the human-development field, men like Dale Carnegie, whose *How to Win Friends and Influence People* was itself highly popular and certainly influenced me in my youth.

Carnegie (1937, 2010) and many others emphasized a "Personality Ethic," showing how to interact with others so as to make them like you and agree with you, techniques that can lead to promotion and popularity.

Covey's review of the "success literature" of the last two centuries convinced him "much of the success literature of the prior 50 years [post-W.W. I] was superficial....filled with social image consciousness, techniques and quick fixes...[but] left the underlying chronic problems untouched to fester and resurface time and again."

This Personality Ethic had two branches: the skillful, sometimes deceitful, management of our public and private relationships and the maintenance of a positive mental attitude.

Covey stressed something very different, a "Character Ethic," following the lead of such thinkers as nineteenth-century New

England essayist Ralph Waldo Emerson who stated, **"What you are shouts so loudly in my ears that I cannot hear what you say."** Covey urged "things like integrity, humility, fidelity, temperance, courage, justice, patience, industry, simplicity, modesty, and the Golden Rule."

The Character Ethic taught that these virtues were necessary for meaningful, satisfying success. The inner determines the outer. "You can't change the fruit without changing the root." The Personality Ethic emphasized techniques designed to put on a successful show. People catch on to phoniness, usually, eventually. At the least, we ourselves know when we have not been authentic.

Covey chose to call his essential principles of successful living "habits," following Aristotle, whom he quoted, **"We are what we repeatedly do.** Excellence, then, is not an act, but a habit." He also quoted educator Horace Mann to the effect that habits are like a rope that is formed by the addition of multiple threads, our regular actions, making it strong.

Covey noted that habits combine the knowledge of what to do and why, with the skill and desire to do them. He then described the seven habits of highly effective people.

Habit 1: Be proactive. To succeed, you need to have vision and then to take action based on it. **Who are you and what do you want to become?** Visualizing your goals will help you reach them, as a compass tells us directions and a beacon draws us to it. The North Star served this purpose for ancient sailors. Knowing True North helps you find the route you need.

Who are you? Having a proper vision of ourselves is difficult. Are you what your genes dictated or what your parents inculcated or what your significant others have demanded? Covey cites author, psychiatrist, Holocaust-survivor Victor Frankl (2006), who wrote he realized in the Nazi concentration camp that he could choose how he viewed himself and his situation and thus how he would allow it to affect him. Four centuries ago, Shakespeare wrote, "for there is nothing good or bad, but thinking makes it so." We can, we do, and we must, choose.

To succeed, we must anticipate, respond, and examine the results of our response to determine its suitability. **How does this apply to writing and publishing your book? If you don't know where you are going, you won't get there.**

Habit 2: Begin with the end in mind. Covey asked his readers to imagine attending their own funeral and ask themselves what they would like to be said about them in the eulogy. What would we want to be remembered for? How would we view our life in retrospect? In the shorter-run, we have projects we undertake that would prosper more fully if we started out with a clear idea of where we wanted them to end. Granted, some undertakings cannot have their outcomes clearly envisaged, but the end results become clearer as the efforts progress.

Without a clear picture of our goals, they are unlikely to be fulfilled. As Diana Ross sang,

Do you know where you're goin' to?

Do you like the things that life is showin' you?

Do you know?

…Now looking back at all we've planned

We let so many dreams just slip through our hands….

You want to write a book, a worthwhile book, one that helps others and helps you. That's where you are going.

Habit 3: Put first things first. Set priorities and keep to your plan to meet them. Covey quoted the great Goethe, German writer and statesman and philosopher, "Things which matter most must never be at the mercy of things which matter least."

Covey asked us to identify one thing we could do regularly now, that we aren't doing, that would make a great difference in our lives. He wrote that leadership is identifying what the "first things" are, and management is seeing that they get done.

Self-management requires self-discipline, a result of exerting your will. Covey urged that we "organize and execute around priorities." To help us, he focused on the urgent, that needing to be done soon, and the important, that contributing to our mission. Concentrate on those things that are important. Try to eliminate, or streamline, your efforts on the unimportant.

You have decided to write your book. Set aside the time and place to do it. Eliminate or at least minimize distractions. Do something to further the project every day.

Habit 4: Think win/win. Make your interactions with others such that both you and they come out ahead, the Golden Rule applied. Set incentives for your team such that cooperation is rewarded, interdependence promoted. In negotiations, aim for "win/win or no deal," and avoid "win/lose," where you benefit and the other does not. In a civil dispute, try to get something for both sides, and resist the temptation to "sue the bums."

Giving in can be inappropriate if you find you have a pattern of "lose/win," yielding when instead you should be sticking up for yourself. A lot of that will leave you resentful and an enabler of bad behavior by others.

Two egotistical types will often let a dispute devolve into "lose/lose," the scorched-earth divorce behavior depicted in the 1989 film classic *The War of the Roses,* in which Michael Douglas and Kathleen Turner wreck what each other values.

Personally, I tend toward "tit-for-tat," or "what goes around comes around," starting by being friendly rather than hostile. Christ taught us to "turn the other cheek," accept injury, but even He drove the money-changers from the temple. Some offenses cannot be ignored.

Covey promoted "win/win or no deal," putting the burden on both sides to take into account the legitimate interests of the other.

You will need the help of others in preparation, publishing, and promoting your book. Make sure their interests are served, too.

Habit 5: Seek first to understand, then to be understood. Covey called communication "the most important skill in life." That dovetails with his belief in the need for interdependence rather than independence. Reading, writing, talking, listening are the four major aspects of communication, and we are trained in all but listening. Often we advise before we understand.

"Most people do not listen with the intent to understand; they listen with the intent to reply....either speaking or preparing to speak....filtering everything through their own paradigms...." In truth, often "where you stand depends on where you sit," what your situation is. Too often we project our view of the world onto what is really rather different. We see the world through the filter of our preconceptions, as the Bible says, "through a glass, darkly. "

Covey chided the father who told him, "I can't understand my kid. He just won't listen to me at all." If you cannot understand your child, it is likely that it is you who has not been listening. We need to listen with the intent to understand before insisting on being understood.

It has been said that communication is the heart of love.

Your book will reflect your ability to understand as well as your ability to communicate. "Seek first to understand...."

Habit 6: Synergize. Synergy is when "the whole is greater than the sum of its parts." Beneficial interactions take place. Creativity increases, as in group brainstorming to solve problems. Cooperation introduces new ways of accomplishing goals. Here, diversity pays off, through specialization, diversification, division of labor, and cooperation.

As you plan and prepare your book, feel free to discuss it with others, either just the subject matter or the entire book project.

Habit 7: Sharpen the saw. To cut wood, sometimes it is more effective to take time out to sharpen the saw, rather than continue to labor with a dull blade. Similarly, in our lives in general, a certain amount of "balanced renewal," Covey's term, is needed: physical, social/emotional, spiritual, and mental. We "sharpen the saw" in these four areas when we exercise and eat more carefully, interact with others empathetically, study and meditate, read and write and plan.

We invest and later spend. Because "the inner determines the outer," self-improvement is of great value.

Some habits are worth acquiring. You will find these seven worth applying to your writing.

CHAPTER 2

PREPARE

I will prepare and someday my chance will come.
Abraham Lincoln

By "prepare," I mean prepare your manuscript. Write, in other words.

BOOK WRITING ADVICE FROM DAN POYNTER (2000)

The advice I'll give comes from a variety of sources, and some from my own experience. Here are a summary and excerpts from **BOOKS: Tips, Stories, & Advice on Writing, Publishing and Promoting**, by Dan Poynter, Para Publishing, Santa Barbara, CA, 2000:

Chapter One: On Writing

- **Typically, four stages:** Rough Draft, Content Edit, Peer Review, and Copy Edit.
- **"Write a page-turner:** get the reader past page eighteen," where most readers never reach. Make chapter one compelling.

- **"Don't allow interruptions** while you are writing." Find a time and place to be left alone.
- **"Take your time."** Books typically take hundreds to a thousand hours to write. Occasionally, however, they have been written within as short a time as three days, for a contest, for example.
- **"Allocate time,"** preferably almost daily. **Amateurs average about a dozen hours per week, but pros average about 30.**
- **"Overcome writers block"** by collecting even more information on your topic. **Write something, almost anything, to get underway.**
- **"Respect your reader's time."** Be pithy, concise, non-repetitive, succinct….
- **"Be precise."** Short sentences, one idea per. Active voice, avoiding prepositional phrases; put subjects and verbs toward the beginning, avoiding trite expressions and jargon.
- **"Combat procrastination."** Do it now.
- **"Write your very best."**
- **"Make your writing compelling."** Inform. Motivate. Entertain.
- **"Make your book worth the money. Size matters."**
- **"Get editorial and design help."**
- **"Know when to call a ghostwriter."** I disagree. Unethical, unless you acknowledge contribution. See discussion below, in Chapter 5.
- **"Do not edit any of the chapters until you Rough Draft the entire book."**
- **"Make the project portable."** Have a manuscript binder. Your laptop computer may serve that purpose.
- **"Fill in the blanks.** The Second Draft is your Content Edit."

- **"Writing is all about re-writing."** As long as your revisions are improvements. At some point, you may introduce more errors than you are catching: diminishing returns have set in.
- **"Know what to cut."** Akin to "know when to hold 'em. Know when to fold 'em."
- **"Be careful of collaborations."** Partnerships are difficult, like marriages. Who is in charge? Who gets what?
- **"Use email. Save time."** Sometimes, use faxes, phone calls.
- **"Get help from experts.** The Third Draft is the peer review."** Send out chapters as you go and eventually send the book draft.
- **"Keep your book to yourself at first."** I prefer that you tell a few close friends, for added commitment and some encouragement.
- **"Check your facts."** Boring, essential.
- **"Hire a copy editor.** The Fourth Draft is the Copy Edit, the cleanup."** You'll be amazed at what you overlooked. Pros are expensive. Good friends with eagle eyes and sharp pencils are almost as useful here.
- **"Know when to call a book doctor."**
- "Hire a proofreader. Do not try to proof your own work."
- **"Use quotations.** Relevant quotations confirm your advice."** Best when near your related words. Familiar quotations are accepted as likely to be true, whether they are or are not. Unfortunately, "the Devil can quote Scripture."
- **"Use anecdotes."** Stories are memorable. Even the *Bible* has parables.
- **"Use humor**....the set-up and the punch line"
- **"Add illustrations.** Say it with pictures."** Sometimes,

however, this is expensive or awkward. Copyright issues can lead to legal hassles.

- **"Combine writing with…."** That is, write while doing something else also. Presumably, this means having a "day job."
- **"Get a computer.** You need the best tools."
- **Consider using speech-recognition software to allow dictating First Draft.** I have benefitted from using Dragon Naturally Speaking for this.
- **"Practice your craft."** Write and re-write.
- **"Set deadlines."** Track your progress. Set some goals.
- **"You are finished when** your manuscript is 98 percent complete—as long as it is 100 percent accurate."
- **"Encourage reader feedback."** Blog some, email some.

I invite you to explore the other material in Poynter's excellent book:

- Chapter Two: Why Write?
- Chapter Three: Why a Book?
- Chapter Four: What to Write
- Chapter Five: Research
- Chapter Six: Build Your Book
- Chapter Seven: Copyright
- Chapter Eight: Finding an Agent, Finding a Publisher
- Chapter Nine: Book Promotion
- Appendix: Your Action Plan

His book includes numerous reference titles, links, and resources. I recommend it highly. For the present, though, stay with me. Let's get on with it: choose your title, at least choose a working title, one you might revise later. Start writing.

GETTING STARTED: SIT. THINK. WRITE. "OPEN A VEIN…"

Gather your stuff and find a place where you won't be disturbed too often. Put your working title at the top of your page. Jot down some elements of an outline. For your memoir: crisis, background, aftermath, significance. For your novel: who, what, when, where, why, and how…the journalist's questions. For your "how to" book: problem, significance, solutions, and resources. You are on your way!

Next, start adding details to the outline. Try the mind-map. Do some writing. Build momentum.

Check the clock. Ideally, you would measure your effort by results, such as word count, or sections completed, but at the very least you can mimic our governments and measure the inputs, your time. Determine to sit there for 30 minutes or even an hour.

Have a goal for your output, or your input. Keep it simple. Keep track.

"Open a vein" if personal revelations or strong, emotive language is needed. Tap your inner comic or your inner tragedian.

MAKING TIME AND SPACE

Finding time is as "easy" as getting up early or turning off the television. The news is repetitious anyway. You've seen sports before. The commercials waste your time. [Aversion therapy for the TV-addicted.] **Finding space requires closing doors or going elsewhere.** These take discipline and practice. I'll show you next how I handled the need for self-discipline toward the beginning of my writing career:

Self-Discipline Exemplified: No Email until Noon

"No email until noon." It is a simple rule, designed to reduce the distractions plaguing this novice freelance writer. A person of stronger character could peruse his email, look only at the most pressing items, and get back to writing. Not me. Better, "Not I."

I established this email rule yesterday. The allowable exceptions are yet to be determined. After I called our printer this morning, I broke it. They had sent me files I really wanted to look at. The files were from a two-page spread in our local weekly paper, with pages 4 and 5 all about Tina and me and my just-finished book, Ting and I: A Memoir of Love, Courage, and Devotion. *I had to read it.*

The paper's editor had given the assignment to a "stringer," a part-time, freelance writer, who herself is a poet and author, Lara Edwards.

"This one is for you" or words to that effect, the editor had said. He did not assign it to the writer who covers our local "beat," town meetings, open-air market openings, etc.

Ms. Edwards, daughter of a highly educated Turkish and American couple, a social worker herself, was the right person to do the piece. She did a magnificent job, breaking the first rule of journalism as practiced today: she read the book before interviewing me. She came prepared, adapted well to our conversation, wrote an article too good for the editor to abridge.

Enough about Lara Edwards, let's talk about me.

Rather than continue writing, I drove down to the printer and arranged to get one hundred copies of the article. Admittedly, I don't have that many friends and family members, but someday I will be sending the copies to people I hope will review the book. I may also hand them out from a stall at a county fair, to entice the rural visitors to buy our book about an interracial couple who have dealt successfully with the challenges of almost twenty years of separation, followed by Tina's increasing disability due to multiple sclerosis. It's upbeat, inspiring. I swear it is.

Now that I am home from the printer, I have resumed writing, by writing this. It is already eleven, which is almost noon. I'll sign off here and check my email.

WRITE THAT BOOK ALREADY!

If you need some more inspiration or some tough love, see Barry and Goldmark (2010), *Write That Book Already!* After giving a list of reasons NOT to become a writer, including desiring: financial security, limelight, structure in your life, free time, not offending your intimates, serving the world, and "hanging around trendy well-dressed people"…none of which you are likely to achieve…they give some advice on getting started: **"Start writing and the muse will come. Not every time, but keep at it….Writing is a discipline, and you have to stay at it,"** like getting in shape by exercising regularly, and, like exercising, it gets easier the more you do.

To get the book written, they suggest, and I quote:

- Concentrate on results.
- Make a to-do list.
- Write down goals.
- Establish a schedule.
- Reward yourself.
- Have someone you trust check your progress.
- Ask for help.
- For inspiration, go to a literary event….
- Break the writing into smaller, more manageable sections.
- Write a chapter outline and then commit yourself to completing each small section.
- Write the book out of order.
- Figure out what works for you.
- If you get stuck, take a walk.

Much of the rest of their book is dedicated to telling would-be authors how to navigate the path to being published by a conventional publisher, although alternatives are discussed. I assume most of my readers are not going this traditional route, as I chose not to.

To write a good book, you need to be able to craft good sentences and paragraphs, topics covered by Strunk and White (1999) in their classic *The Elements of Style*.

WRITING BASICS: *THE ELEMENTS OF STYLE* (STRUNK & WHITE, 1999)

Communication is at the heart of human relationships: reading, writing, speaking, listening.

"Writing means sharing. It's part of the human condition to want to share things—thoughts, ideas, opinions," wrote Brazilian novelist Paulo Coelho.

Use care: what you write often impacts others much more and lasts far longer than what you say. How well you write influences the opinions of others about you.

I describe here a valuable and inexpensive little book [only 105 pages long] that will help you write better and avoid the most common mistakes. Originally written and published a century ago by Cornell University Professor William Strunk, Jr., and updated decades later by E.B. White, this classic text on writing, *The Elements of Style,* has guided myriads of writers and editors through the thickets of English usage, grammar, and form.

Here are excerpts from Strunk and White's "little book," with its original words in **boldface,** followed by my own examples in italics and by my comments**:**

I. ELEMENTARY RULES OF USAGE

1. **Form the possessive singular of nouns by adding 's.**

A dog's life, Tom's pen, and Charles's paper are right. Note that possessives of plurals that themselves end in s take only the apostrophe, so we have: *several friends' birthdays.* Plurals not ending in s do take 's: *the children's hour.*

2. **In a series of three of more terms with a single conjunction, use a comma after each term except the last.**

This, that, and the other all qualify.

3. Enclose parenthetic expressions between commas.

It is best, at least most of the time, to avoid parentheses.

4. Place a comma before a conjunction introducing a co-ordinate clause.

This is often done incorrectly, but it is important.

5. Do not join independent clauses by a comma.

This is also often done incorrectly; it is important to use a semi-colon instead or start a new sentence.

6. Do not break sentences in two.

Be sure. Not to. Or only rarely!

7. A participial phrase at the beginning of a sentence must refer to the grammatical subject.

Trying to write well, you should heed this rule.

II. ELEMENTARY PRINCIPLES OF COMPOSITION

8. Make the paragraph the unit of composition: one paragraph to each topic.

This can be tricky, as "topic" is a slippery term. Lately, short paragraphs have become fashionable, and they are effective.

9. **As a rule, begin each paragraph with a topic sentence; end it in conformity with the beginning.**

"In conformity" does not mean repeating, however. Be more creative as you restate.

10. **Use the active voice.**

Active: *She wrote the poem.* Passive: *The poem was written by her.*

11. **Put statements in positive form.**

Do not put statements in this negative form, generally.

12. **Use definite, specific, concrete language.**

As done in "connecting Asian American women to the world," the slogan of asiancemagazine.com, where I publish monthly.

13. **Omit needless words.**

Be pithy, terse, and succinct, avoiding repetition and redundancy, unlike this sentence.

14. **Avoid a succession of loose sentences.**

Loose sentences are distinguished from periodic ones, where the main idea comes at the end.

15. **Express co-ordinate ideas in similar form.**

Use parallelism in sentence structure: *she wrote the book, and he drew the pictures.*

16. Keep related words together.

Make it clear what your modifiers modify.

17. In summaries, keep to one tense.

Generally, use the simple present or simple past tense: *it does, it did....*

18. Place the emphatic words of a sentence at the end.

Easier said than done.

III. A FEW MATTERS OF FORM

Here the authors advise the writer on: colloquialisms, exclamations, headings, hyphens, margins, numerals, parentheses, quotations, references, syllabication, and titles.

IV. WORDS AND EXPRESSIONS COMMONLY MISUSED

Strunk and White (1999) dissect over 100 troublesome words and phrases, such as distinguishing "disinterested" versus "uninterested."

V. AN APPROACH TO STYLE

1. Place yourself in the background.

Unless, of course, you are writing a memoir or autobiography. Even then, try not to brag nor whine.

2. Write in a way that comes naturally.

Write pretty much as you talk.

3. Work from a suitable design.

An outline will help greatly. In a formal piece, your first paragraph should outline the presentation such that each sentence could be a suitable topic sentence for a paragraph in the body of the work that follows.

4. Write with nouns and verbs.

Use specific nouns and descriptive verbs.

5. Revise and rewrite.

You will always find something worth improving; however, don't let perfectionism cripple you.

6. Do not overwrite.

Avoid grandiosity, flowery words, highly complicated and "literary" sentences.

7. Do not overstate.

Understate, rather than overstate. Suggest, unless you can justly claim. Occasionally, be subtle. Shakespeare wrote, "by indirections find directions out." Don't sacrifice clarity, however.

8. Avoid the use of qualifiers.

Specific nouns rarely need adjectives. Apt verbs don't need adverbs.

9. Do not affect a breezy manner.

10. Use orthodox spelling.

11. Do not explain too much.

While good advice for fiction, much nonfiction does need careful elucidation. Others have advised writers to "show not tell." My writing partner, Kathleen Blake Shields, does not write that her aunt Lila is a prickly curmudgeon; rather, Kathy gives two anecdotes about Aunt Lila:

Aunt Lila was taken out to a fancy restaurant in our neighborhood. She was served the usual courses: salad, entrée, soup, dessert. She was not wholly pleased, however. She called the waiter over and said to him, "Tell the chef that I make my soup at home just like he made this, but I add only one can of water."

Not-so-lovable Aunt Lila watched the firemen attack with hoses and axes a fire that had started in her house. She was unhappy with their methods. She told the Chief, "You can stop what you're doing now, and I'll save the foundation."

12. Do not construct awkward adverbs.

Don't be adverbially challenged.

13. Make sure the reader knows who is speaking.

In fiction, the dialogue and attribution ("Jill said") should make this clear. In nonfiction, your facts and opinions need to be distinguished from those of others.

14. Avoid fancy words.

Eschew sesquipedalianism. Keep your words simple, usually.

15. Do not use dialect unless your ear is good.

16. Be clear.

If "brevity is the soul of wit," clarity should be the goal of wit.

17. Do not inject opinion.

Editorials and persuasive pieces of various types are allowed to violate this recommendation.

18. Use figures of speech sparingly.

Occasional similes and metaphors spice your prose, but they should not comprise the main course.

19. Do not take shortcuts at the cost of clarity.

U no wat ths means, prbbly.

20. Avoid foreign languages.

Having to look up a foreign term is my *bete noire.*

21. Prefer the standard to the offbeat.

This is the same advice I'd give my nieces about dating!

To repeat, get *The Elements of Style.*

HIRE AN EDITOR

That's not an advertisement for my services. Many authors of books advising would-be authors strongly recommend that you not rely on yourself to edit your work after you have gotten it written to your satisfaction. Before you turn it over, Karia (2015) recommends you do the first edit yourself:

- **Make structural changes:** move things around if necessary
- **Adjust the tone**
- **Cut out irrelevant ideas**
- **Add personality**
- **Break up paragraphs**
- **Correct grammar**
- **Add important content**
- **Add summaries at end of chapters, "In a Nutshell."**

FIGURES OF SPEECH

Figures of speech sparingly used can improve our writing.

A **figure of speech** is a nonliteral use of the language to achieve a special effect. Three very common ones are simile, metaphor, and hyperbole.

A **simile** is a figure of speech making an explicit comparison between things, usually using the words "like" or "as." A fine example comes from Mark Hazard's detective novel *Corus and the Case of the Chaos:* "Chief Detective Corus slapped the aging vending machine. The bag of chips he'd paid seventy-five cents for clung to the mechanism *like a kid on the monkey bars,* taunting him." I've italicized his graphic simile. By the way, "Mark Hazard" is a great name for a mystery writer. Was he born with it? Just asking.

A **metaphor** is an implicit comparison. "John *slithered* away." John hasn't exactly been called a snake, but we get the idea.

Hyperbole is deliberate gross exaggeration. "I'm so hungry I could eat a horse." Occasionally there's horsemeat in the burgers, but that's another story.

NONFICTION BOOKS: THE TRUTH, APPROXIMATELY

Books, even the best ones, only approximate reality. Not all details can be included. Not all details are correct. Even so, the nonfiction book author tries to include the important aspects and get these right. Ideally, the sources for the "facts" will be made clear, allowing some checking by skeptical readers and allowing others to follow up and get more information.

Experts have been shown to be wrong with surprising frequency (see David H. Freedman's 2010 book *Wrong*), so you will be in good company if some of what you write turns out not to be correct. Try to keep that to a minimum!

CHOOSING YOUR NONFICTION NICHE

In his *How to Write a Non-Fiction Kindle eBook in 15 Days*, Karia (2015) recommends you first explore your interests and knowledge:

- **What do I know well?**

- **What am I interested in?**
- **What could I research effectively?**
- **What experts can I access easily?**

For *Write Your Book with Me,* I knew how to write, had written and published a lot, am interested in writing, and the Internet gives lots of opportunities for obtaining more information, as does amazon.com. I accessed the experts through their books. For my memoir, *Ting and I,* the answers were clear: I knew our life. For a third book, Our *How to Manage Nursing Care at Home* I had over a decade of experience and co-authored it with Diane R. Beggin, a very smart and articulate Registered Nurse who had even more experience along with the requisite professional training and credentials. For a fourth book, *SOLVED! Curing Your Medical Insurance Problems,* I had a co-author, Adria Goldman Gross, who was an expert in the field, and I supplied some personal experience plus coaching and editing.

But will anyone buy it? I didn't care much about sales with my memoir, as it was largely a gift to my wife and my family and friends. I hoped this book on writing would be popular and helpful, but at least it would be useful for my writing students / clients, and it serves as a thick business card. **One author claimed that books are the best business cards on Earth.** Still, one would like to go beyond handing them out.

Karia (2015) and others recommend using amazon.com to explore what is selling and where the opportunities are. He recommends noting the books that have sales ranks of 20,000 or less (where lower means more sales). **A book of his that was ranked near 10,000 was selling 200 to 300 ebooks per month.** A book ranking near 200,000 would be selling about one-twentieth as many per month. He notes, "If you can't find at least three books with that low sales rank [10.000], it means there isn't much demand for your topic." Move on, unless you don't care about sales. Karia also recommends checking with udemy.com to see what courses are most popular.

Next, focus on "narrowing your niche." My title here, *Write Your Book with Me,* is probably too broad. "Memoir" rather than "Book" might have been better, but it would not have reflected the title of my web site and would have narrowed the book's scope too greatly. "Bestseller" would have been even more attractive, but I cannot really promise that. "First Book" would have narrowed the field and indicated that I was going to help newbies who were not likely to get published by traditional publishers. Our *How to Manage Nursing Care at Home* seems both needed and manageable, though. Watch for it on the bestsellers lists…if there's nothing better to watch on TV.

More market research can be obtained by reviewing the Amazon reviews of the books you might have written.

CHOOSING YOUR NONFICTION TITLE

Authors understand that getting people to read our books is almost like seduction: we lure them in with a good-looking cover, capture their interest with our title, then we tell our story.

Let's say you have chosen to write a nonfiction book. You have picked your topic. Next, you'll want to have a working title, one that you may change in the future, but something that allows you to refer to the book comfortably.

Taking some time and effort to choose your title makes sense. This will help guide the direction of your writing. If you find later on that you have strayed, you can then decide whether to change the title or to bring your writing back in line with your original idea.

As you will see in what follows, there are some sound suggestions for developing a title that will help your book reach its audience. You'll be balancing between what is creative and what is clear. In some cases your title may be a bit mysterious, but you will choose to clarify with a subtitle.

Your book's formal title may be different from the "nickname" you started with, your working title. No problem.

Writing coach Kristen Eckstein (2013) has written a fine short book, a bargain on amazon.com at $0.99 for the Kindle version: *AUTHOR'S QUICK GUIDE to Creating a Killer Non-fiction Book Title,* one of her series of GUIDES. I'll summarize some of it here, and explore how it applied to my own memoir, but I also encourage you to buy her book.

I titled my memoir of our 50-year-long interracial marriage *Ting and I: A Memoir of Love, Courage, and Devotion.* Let's analyze this in the light of **Ms. Eckstein's prescriptions:**

1. **The primary title** is *Ting and I.* Unless you are well-known, you are advised to **keep your title short, five words or less.** Done. Who is "Ting"? My wife, born Su Ting-ting. "Ting" added a touch of mystery, a good thing, and perhaps echoed the familiar movie *The King and I,* another good thing. It sounded foreign, which is exotic

to some and attractive, but off-putting to others, so the result is mixed. Women buy more books than men, so it would have been nice if this suggested that "Ting" is indeed a woman, but it doesn't. Can't win 'em all.

2. My *Ting and I*'s **subtitle** is *A Memoir of Love, Courage, and Devotion.* **It tells you what kind of book it is, a memoir, which is good.** Check. It does not exactly indicate **what benefit the reader will get**, though some might enjoy reading about love, courage, and devotion, and some may even be inspired.

3. The title does not indicate **how to do something,** and **How To is a favorite category for book buyers.** Perhaps reading the book will show you how a very lovable person (my wife, Tina) behaves, but the title and sub-title don't indicate that. Oh, well.

4. The title lacks **numbers, which are often very attention-getting:** *7 Habits of Highly Effective People, One-Minute Manager, 50 Shades of Grey.* A number is specific, almost a promise.

5. The title and subtitle were not chosen for **Search Engine Optimization [SEO],** but sometimes one should do so. You can find lots of material on SEO, but you will have a real challenge to stand out, unless you have picked a very small niche.

Karen Eckstein's handy GUIDE includes a link to her coaching site, UltimateBookCoach.com, and a link for a free set of instructions, "**The 50 Ultimate Book Titles Template**," with suggestions for creating your own killer, ultimate, maximally effective title. Hmm, "The 50 Ultimate…" seems like she took her own advice.

For fiction titles, you have more latitude, but some of the same rules apply. *Moby Dick? The Sun Also Rises? Tender is the Night? To Kill a Mockingbird?* Could you guess their themes? Talent trumps titles.

Ebook success Karia (2105) gives the following advice, prefer:

- **Short title** with explanatory sub-title
- **Keywords** likely to be used in searches
- Title that indicates **benefits**
- Title that raises **curiosity**

I think *Ting and I: A Memoir of Love, Courage, and Devotion,* fell short on promising benefits. Our *How to Manage Nursing Care at Home* seems to fit all the above except "curiosity."

Karia (2015) cites Craig Valentine's book *World Class Speaking,* for this **mnemonic summary, EDGE, for benefits:**

- **E**steem (more): gain prestige, confidence
- **D**o more: improve your abilities and performance
- **G**ain more: money, friends, time...
- **E**njoy more: be happier, worry less

Your title should offer some of the above. Ask others for their suggestions. If you have a significant Social Media following (Twitter, Facebook, email), you can try "A/B comparisons," soliciting votes on which title (A or B) they prefer. You can spend money on Facebook ads and make A/B comparisons with Clickthroughs or Likes as the metric. Later on here, I discuss my generally successful experience with Facebook ads.

YOU *CAN* SELL A BOOK BY ITS COVER (ALMOST)

Here I quote and paraphrase indie author Rayne Hall (2015), who has written about the 20 elements she believes may hinder your book from selling or may help it sell. **First, you need an effective cover:**

Most book purchases—ebooks or print—happen online. The reader browsing sites sees a dozen or more books displayed on the page. Her eye scans over them, and unless one catches her attention, she clicks 'next'.... **Your book cover has a fraction of a second to arrest the eye.**

- What else? For one thing **symmetrical designs**, where the left side is essentially the mirror image of the right side, **are not as attention-getting as asymmetrical designs.** Hall gives several graphic examples, and it is clear that the more complex asymmetrical designs tend to be more eye-catching.
- Although you are not likely to do your own cover designing, it is good to know some basic principles. For example, Hall recommends dividing the front cover region into thirds, left and right, top and bottom, a pattern similar to the hashmark # or tic-tac-toe pattern. **Arrange to have the main graphic element be off-center. Align the author name to one side and book title to another.** "If possible, arrange the title on one of the two horizontal lines, and an arresting part of the picture where two lines cross."
- Especially for online sales, where the cover is seen as a little "thumbnail," **simplicity is preferable to complexity,** as much detail will be lost anyway. **People get our attention.** "A character attracts the eye more than a landscape

or an object. A portrait or half-body character (from the waist up) typically gets more attention than a full-body figure." If consistent with your genre, use a single figure or object.

- Because of the size reduction for online display, much **text will be hard to read unless the font size is quite large. Title and author, two elements, are generally better than three or four.** If you're not famous, making your name particularly large will not likely fool most potential buyers, however.
- **Make sure that your cover signals the reader what genre it represents.** Look at other competitor covers to get a good general idea. Beware getting stock photos or illustrations already used by other book covers, as this can confuse the reader, perhaps annoying her.
- **Covers with few colors are more effective than those with many.** Strong contrasts, in color, shade, and light-and-dark attract the eye.

Ebook maven Karia (2015) joins the chorus of those who stress the importance of an attractive cover. He changed one of his and tripled his sales rate by doing so. Actually, he got an artist to do it, as he warns **"Don't Do It Yourself!"** That does not keep him from having opinions about what works, however:

- **Title**: large, so as to be readable when in Amazon thumbnail
- **Contrasting colors**: for legibility
- **Visual simplicity**: again, consider what the "thumbnail" will look like

Karia joins others who recommend **fiverr.com** as a source for book-cover designers. Have several do several, then select one. You should search for images on **shutterstock.com** to indicate what you are seeking. He gives detailed advice on working with these graphic artists. **"Remember that your cover is one of the most important parts of your book."**

Why, then, did I almost choose a plain cover for this book, WYBWM? The three paperback options my publisher offers that I was considering include various features, only some of which I care about. A plain cover with a big title and my name is part of the $400 package. Next more expensive, at about $700, would include a picture on the cover, and most of my writers get this one or the next more expensive at about $1000 that includes an artistic cover. Being married, I am spending not just "my" money, but "our" money, and I hate to waste it. The book may become popular, but may merely become a "thick business card." I can handle only a limited number of new writing partners, anyway. If I make *WYBWM* into blog pieces or videos, the original cover won't mean much. Finally, one would like to think, perhaps foolishly, that his book is bought for its contents not its cover. Oh, no, extinguish the ego! I bought the fancy cover.

DON'T BLOW THE BLURB

Hall (2015) claims:

The blurb (book description) on the book's back cover and on-line product page is the most important part of the book. Almost everyone reads or at least scans it before deciding whether or not to buy. It probably plays a bigger role in your sales than any other factor.

- For nonfiction blurbs, emphasize reader benefits. For fiction, emphasize the plot.
- How to optimize the blurb? Hall urges you to **keep it short, 200-300 words. Be pithy. Use vivid verbs and specific nouns.** Some genres have "thrill words." Keep it simple: in fiction, the hero's goal and a conflict. Don't tell much of the plot, tease the reader, instead. Emotion overwhelms reason. Acton trumps contemplation. **Hall's formula: "[Character] needs [goal] before [deadline]; otherwise, [drastic consequences]."** Penniless author needs bestseller by year-end, or his long-suffering fiancée walks? Yes!
- Having written some over-long blurbs herself, Hall concluded, **"Readers don't want to read long blurbs. They want to read books."** Make them want to read yours.

HOW TO WRITE A BOOK FROM OUTLINE TO FINISH LINE (HITZ, 2015)

With a name like "Hitz" it's got to be good. It is. And I got it for free at amazon.com.

Ms. Hitz's subtitle is **"10 Simple Ways to Outline Your Nonfiction Book."** Here they are:

- Whiteboard
- Mind Mapping Software [FreeMind, free software]
- Sticky Notes
- Evernote [includes dictation and can be used on mobile devices]
- Trello [software for note-taking and arranging]
- Scrivener

- **Pen and paper**
- **PowerPoint Slides [from prior presentations]**
- **Blog Posts [recycle your stuff]**
- **Podcast Episodes [if you've done some]**

She gives useful links for several of these, as well. She particularly likes Evernote and Scrivener, as do many other writers.

Ms. Hitz (2015) follows up with **"three ways to write your book":**

- **Write it in Chunks of Time**
- **Speak Your Book**
- **Hire a Ghostwriter**

Setting aside "chunks of time" can work for many writers, especially those with "day jobs." Dictation speeds easily exceed those of most typists, and several dictation apps and programs are listed. I discuss ghostwriters later here, but she has some valuable advice on working with them, too.

She lists 40+ tools she uses almost every day at her site **shelley-hitz.com,** which has much additional useful material.

Outlining your nonfiction book can be easy. Hitz suggests:

- **Introduction:** emphasize the benefits of your book.
- **Chapter One:** start with a personal story…situation… turning point…resolution…outcome.
- **Main Chapters:** fill in the details.
- **Conclusion:** summarize book, tell what you learned.

This is a variation on the classic advice given to public speakers: **"tell them what you'll say; say it; tell them what you said."**

Even before the reader gets to your Chapter One, however, much happens ahead of it, discussed next.

WHAT'S UP FRONT COUNTS: DEDICATION, TABLE OF CONTENTS, ACKNOWLEDGMENTS, FOREWORD, PREFACE

"This is dedicated to the one I love…" so began a popular song a few decades ago. That opening line caught the listener's attention, and your **Dedication** page can likewise capture your reader's notice.

Judy Axtell dedicated *But…at What Cost,* her memoir-plus-political-tract, "To Frederick Douglass and his deep understanding of human nature and freedom," celebrating a great African-American and alerting her readers that she is not the stereotype they have when they think of conservatives.

The dedication of my *Ting and I:* *A Memoir of Love, Courage, and Devotion* goes:

Offered with love to Tina Su Cooper, the light of my life

Love one another, but make not a bond of love:
Let it rather be a moving sea between the shores of your souls.

Give your hearts, but not into each other's keeping
For only the hand of Life can contain your hearts.

—Khalil Gibran, *The Prophet*

All that we love deeply becomes part of us.

—Helen Keller

From the dedication, the reader knows immediately that this is a story about a deep and long-lasting love that has endured, among other things, long separation.

The dedication to *Kidnapped Twice: Then Betrayed and Abused,* by Mary E. Seaman and myself, is simply, "To those who care deeply about the treatment of the least powerful among us: our children, our pets, and our wildlife." It tells you a lot, favorably, about Mary right away.

One more example: novelist Mark Hazard (2015) dedicates his *Corus and the Case of the Chaos: A Detective Mystery,* "**For Rudy. Best dog ever.**" It does not necessarily indicate Hazard lacks friends and family. Rather, it sets up the novel's theme: a master detective struggling with depression triggered by the death of his beloved dog.

Your **Table of Contents** can pique the reader's interest, help the reader know what to expect, make it easy to find material within the book if there is no index, and often will show up in brief descriptions of the book, such as Amazon's Inside the Book feature.

Your **Acknowledgments** give you the opportunity to thank those who have contributed to your life and to your book. What a nice way to thank them! Whom you praise may add to your credibility and *gravitas*.

The **Foreword** should be written by someone who likes what you have written, says so, and has credibility because of position and accomplishments.

Your **Preface** lets you tell your readers why you wrote the book and why it is likely to be of value to them.

Not all books will have all these elements, but most should.

With these out of the way, we move on to your **Introduction.**

WRITING A COMPELLING NONFICTION INTRODUCTION

We'll explore some options for your introduction, which options will be different for the different nonfiction genres.

First, "how to" book introductions are discussed.

Given that the popular topics of health, wealth, and personal relationships are all susceptible to the "how to" treatment, this approach covers a lot of ground. After the introduction, you will go into much more detail on why and how. Memoirs need a different approach, discussed after this.

8 Steps to a Compelling "How To" Book Introduction

This is based on an excellent Amazon Kindle ebook, *Book Launch*, by highly successful writer and publisher Chandler Bolt and co-author J. Roper. The book is subtitled "How to write, market, and self-publish your first bestseller in 3 months or less AND use it to start and grow a six-figure income." Modest claims rarely sell books.

Bolt notes that number-one bookseller amazon.com gives the first 10% of the book in its "Inside the Book" feature, so your Table of Contents and your Introduction need to grab the reader.

Here are Bolt's eight steps:

1. **Identify the problem.** Let the reader know what problem you will be solving.
2. **Present the solution briefly.** Your book will show how to solve the problem by....
3. **Reassert your credibility.** Tell who you are and why you wrote the book and why your advice should be trusted.
4. **Restate the benefits.** Tell reader what they will get, again, in more detail.
5. **Give them proof.** Tell some stories, briefly.
6. **Make a promise.** Bigger is better, as long as you deliver.
7. **Warn against waiting.** If they wait, they may lose out on benefits.
8. **Get them to start reading immediately.** Read it now, to be ready whenever.

Chandler Bolt's book is packed with useful information and serves as an effective advertisement for his training program: www.self-publishingschool.com. Adria Goldman Gross and I used this outline to introduce our book (Gross & Cooper, 2015) on reducing medical billing and re-imbursement errors.

Writing a Riveting Introduction to Your Memoir

If you need some introductory material, perhaps it is best to place it in your preface. **The introduction to your memoir should be something dramatic, something to engage the reader, probably**

a crisis in your life of some sort. Ideally, the reader would have to go farther in the book to find the resolution of the crisis, so this first introductory material ends with a natural cliff-hanger.

You are going to follow this crisis section with a description of what led up to the crisis. After that, describe the resolution, if any, and the lessons to be learned from your experience. You may choose to include added material, such as references that will be of help to the reader.

NONFICTION: FACTS AND OPINIONS

We distinguish fiction from nonfiction, the latter intended to be literally true, whereas fiction tells its truths through skillful lies that we may choose to accept through the "willing suspension of our disbelief."

Popular forms of nonfiction books include how-to, travel, cooking, biography and memoir, and efforts at persuasion…some of which efforts are more fiction than fact.

There are nearly infinite facts to choose from, so opinions based on facts can still vary widely. "That's why we have horse races," the saying goes, because one's predictions must be confirmed by testing. Many a bettor has had to revise his evaluation technique.

"Where you stand depends on where you sit," because the information you have will differ from what others have and what you have at stake will differ also. The memoir is particularly subjective.

MEMOIRS: PART OF THE TRUTH, HOW YOU SAW IT

A memoir is a story about your life, as you saw it, as you understood it. It is less formal than an autobiography or a biography. It tells the truth, not necessarily all the truth. Reasons for writing a memoir include:

1. **Self-understanding:** Some facts will speak for themselves. Some will need interpretation. Some will reveal what was unclear to you then. Some will give you more insight into yourself and those who influenced you.
2. **Explanations to others:** Your audience can be your spouse, your family, your friends, neighbors, colleagues, even the world. You had reasons for the choices you made. Explain them. You learned from the outcomes. Share those lessons. You may want to take credit or accept blame. Do so.
3. **History:** You will not be available forever to tell the stories that deserve to be told. Your memoir lives on. You may choose to add some leaves and blossoms to the bare branches of your family tree. An occasional knot-hole or broken limb may deserve mentioning and explanation. A bad apple may fail to make the grade.
4. **Thanks.** You want to thank publicly and at length those who have enriched your life. Our memoir thanked those who have saved my wife's life and helped keep her alive.
5. **Money**? Writing a memoir is buying a ticket to a lottery. You need to WHIP up an audience:

   -- **W**rite well;
   -- have a **H**ook;
   -- offer **I**nsight;
   -- promote via a **P**latform.

I gave away more copies of my *Ting and I* memoir than I sold, despite having some fine reviews at amazon.com.

A downside to memoir-writing is the loss of privacy entailed. In her book *Writing the Memoir*, Judith Barrington described the conflict the memoirist faces in choosing between privacy and openness:

"As soon as I started to write about my own life, I understood that to speak honestly about family and community is to step way out of line, to risk accusations of betrayal, and to shoulder the burden of being the one who blows the whistle on the myths that families and communities create to protect themselves from painful truths. This threat was like a great shadow lurking at the corner of my vision, as it is for anyone who approaches this task, even before the writing leads them into sticky territory.

I was molded into a pursuer of truth by my times. Active in the early feminist movement and shaped by the conscious-ness-raising that insisted on scrupulously examined lives, I was challenged in my 20s to take a second look, and then a third and fourth one, at the facts of my life....

By demanding our "loyalty" in the form of silence, some of the people we are closest to have coerced us into collaborating with lies and myths. We cannot, however, respond to this coercion by rushing angrily into print. We must examine our responsibil-ity as writers to those we write about, even while holding fast to our truths."

You will be praised by some and resented by some.

British author Victoria Twead (2013) penned a very favorably reviewed 40-page work, *How to Write a Bestselling Memoir: Three Steps To Success.* Her three steps are: **write, publish, and promote**.

Write:

- She recommends using a **pen name**, rather than your own, unless you are a celebrity. If your book becomes popular, you may not want the attention on yourself and your family. Then again, you may find it useful.
- **Short, punchy titles** sell better than long ones. Your subtitle can explain the possibly puzzling title. She cites *Eat, Pray, Love,* an exceptionally successful memoir. Include a keyword or two, to help your reader find you on the Internet.
- Map out your timeline on a big sheet of paper and start filling in details. You may have the book itself start at a dramatic part of your life rather than your youth. Plan where you will finish, too.
- **First chapter** is most important, as those who sample the book will start there.
- **Last chapter** will leave final impressions with those who might write reviews.
- **Chapter lengths:** a matter of taste, but about 2500 words (10 pages) suits her well.
- **Tell the truth**, not all of it. Change names as seems wise. Alert the reader to that.
- **Make every word count.**
- **Keep paragraphs short.**
- **Use cliff-hangers to keep readers intrigued.** Describe event, but leave consequences for later chapter, with some recap.

- **Dialogue** "is the perfect tool to build characters and develop them." It is "easy to read and increases the pace." Unfortunately, you rarely know it with accuracy in retrospect. Final punctuation occurs within the quotation marks, and each new speaker gets new paragraph.
- **Vocabulary** should be varied. Use synonyms. Twead favors using a thesaurus, but other authors have maintained that if the word is not in your usual vocabulary, eschew it. "Never try to be too clever by using unfamiliar words." Be alert to too much repetition.
- **Proofreading** requires great care. Print out the material. Go line by line with a ruler. Get friends and family to help proof, if you can. Pay a pro if need be. "I am always horrified by the number of typos that are found by the professional when I thought I'd checked every word meticulously….typos still appear in even the most professional, traditionally published books." Life goes on. Some are appalled.
- **Size matters:** Twead finds 50,000 to 100,000 words best, in terms of reader acceptance. "…between 75,000 and 95,000 words is probably ideal."

Publish:

- **Traditional:** The publishing house pays you, takes the risk, calls the shots, edits, proofreads, promotes a bit. You book may make it into bookstores. To get there, you will need an agent, query letters, the whole rigmarole, which she describes. Readers of my book, *WYBWM,* are not likely to take this route.
- **Self-publishing:** You do the work, get most of the profits, if any.

- **Vanity press:** Also known as "subsidy" press, they will do much of the work, publish almost anything, and promote it minimally. Twead dislikes them intensely. I have been happy with Outskirts Press.
- **Independent press:** Unlike subsidy or vanity press, they do not charge the author and are selective. Twead likes her Ant Press.
- **Front cover:** Want a stunning one: colored background, large font, and simple design, professional. Twead gives technical details for ebook and paperback book covers.
- **Back cover:** Your **blurb**, or teaser, is crucial, the hook to catch the reader. Write in third person, set scene, create curiosity. Add praise from others, if you have some. Awards? Bio?
- **Front matter:** I cover this elsewhere.
- **Text format:** Details for those who are self-publishing.

50 Promotion tips: Includes distribute free review copies early, have a website, start a blog, Facebook, answer comments from others, Tweet on Twitter, join Google+, participate in forums, Shelfari, Goodreads, Librarything, giveaways, visit local bookstores and see if they will let you hold a signing, contact local papers and radio stations, collect email addresses, start a newsletter, get business cards, write articles and press releases, make a two-minute video, tailor your email signature, create flyers and bookmarks, offer to speak, donate books to local libraries and charitable groups, sell at flea markets, rent a billboard, print on favors like mugs, and "…the very best way to sell books is to write another."

Victoria Twead's book sells for $4 as Amazon Kindle ebook and $8 as a paperback.

In their excellent *You Should* Really *Write a Book*, Regina Brooks and Brenda Lane Richardson put memoirs into six categories:

1. Coming-of-Age Memoirs
2. Addiction and Compulsion Memoirs
3. Transformation Memoirs
4. Travel and Food Memoirs
5. Religion and Spirituality Memoirs
6. Outlier Subgenres

Coming-of-Age

They write, "It has been said that **the only good thing that ever came from having bad parents is that they make good memoirs."** This is a subset of the rule that "bad times make good stories," or at least make interesting stories. Sadly, lots of sad stories exist, such as the memoir by Mary E. Seaman and myself, *Kidnapped Twice: Then Betrayed and Abused.* Though published right before Christmas, the book could not be promoted then as likely to contribute to holiday cheer.

Fortunately, happy memoirs exist, too, such as our *High Shoes and Bloomers* by Alice Conner Selfridge (2014) and our *Home Is Where the Story Begins* by Kathleen Blake Shields (2015), both books being fine fare for holiday giving.

Addiction and Compulsion

Brooks and Richardson note that more than an eighth of the population is addicted to drugs or alcohol, and many celebrities are in this group. I reviewed for Amazon a memoir, *Needle,* by a recovering addict, and I found little to like. If the addict takes responsibility and cleans up his act, well and good. If we just get a series of excuses, what does that contribute? Still, such books sell, and the descent and recovery make a natural story arc, like a U. These are what were once called "cautionary tales," though some authors seem to revel in the celebrity that attends them. B & R have a how-to section on writing these.

Transformation or Survivor

The more harrowing the better; the more dramatic the crisis, the more impressive the survival, and one had better learn something from the experience. You get the idea. B & R give lots of good advice. See them for it. **The best of the books** in the sub-genres in this category all share: **inevitability** of something terrible survived, **bonding** between the reader and the author, **suspense, character development, victimization, empathy, and insight.** The down side of such works is that the situations the protagonists are in often disgust the reader, unless leavened with humor and fascinating unique details and unless the author is capable of getting the readers immediately and deeply involved.

The variety of perilous personal predicaments as memoir material astounds. I'm partial to *The Diving Bell and the Butterfly: A Memoir of Life in Death*, written by Jean-Dominque Bauby (1997), paralyzed to such a degree by the neurological "locked-in syndrome," that he communicated his memoir to a patient nurse-secretary by blinking his left eye. Shortly after the book was done, he gave up the ghost. Suffice it to say, your difficulties in writing your book will pale in comparison with *Monsieur* Bauby's. Take heart from that.

Travel and Food

Yes, I know travel books and cooking books are popular, but I have little taste for them. Brooks and Richardson report what publishers are looking for, and here I summarize: **a protagonist with a strong desire, who is opinionated and fairly outspoken, likeable, capable of describing the sensory experiences (seeing, hearing, smelling, tasting, feeling), who uncovers unfamiliar aspects of the locale, giving historical and cultural context, with both a strong story line and an insightful interior monologue, ending the journey with a transformation, growth, and some lessons** for the rest of us. Easy, right? Just don't forget to have a plot! And add some humor.

Again, see B & R for lots of detailed advice. Later.

I cannot advise you on food memoirs. I am on a rather restricted diet, and the subject of food, especially exotic food, either nauseates me or bores me or both. My usual dinner fare is meat and salad, lots of dressing, hold the carbs. Some live to eat. I eat to live.

Still, "each to his own taste," or as the Romans said: *de gustibus non est disputandum*.

Religion and Spirituality

This topic needs to be handled with great care. Politics and religion are explosive. Because of its great importance, religion is often a source of heated contention; unfortunately, one person's allegory or parable is another's literal truth. There is a large market for books about God and about religious experiences. Over $1 billion a year is spent on such books in the U.S. alone.

A classic in the genre is Thomas Merton's (1948, 1978) *The Seven-Storey Mountain,* his struggle in the World War II era to find God. B & R summarize a plethora of religious memoirs.

Outlier Subgenres

Brooks and Richardson list: biblio, canine, comedic, family saga, gardening, grief, incarceration, information-based, parenting, romance, venture. They describe each in detail. As is often written in reference lists, *op. cit.;* see the B & R book itself.

Regardless of the memoir genre, Judith Barrington advised memoirists:

Your reader has to be willing to be both entertained by the story itself and interested in how you now, looking back on it, understand it.

In order for the reader to care about what you make of your life, there has to be an engaging voice in the writing—a voice that captures the personality. In all kinds of informal essays including the memoir, the voice is conversational.

To keep the voice "conversational," you will write in the first person, using "I" and "we" to refer to yourself as the subject of your sentences. When talking to others about your book, you would often indicate, "the narrator…." Thus, you might tell a friend, "I chose to have the narrator make that information public." You will sound quite author-like, and you are becoming one.

Judith Barrington advises that we lose our reluctance to make judgments, as these spice the memoir and add value. Because the "other side" does not get to answer, however, try to be fair and even to indicate what the other point of view might be.

Knowing what you want to write about includes knowing what to leave out. "To be effective, be selective." To make a point, an example or two will suffice; more will bore.

Barrington warns us to avoid special pleading:

The tone of such pieces may be serious, ironic, angry, sad, or almost anything except whiny. There must be no hidden plea for help—no subtle seeking out of sympathy. The writer must have done her work, made her peace with the past, and have been telling the story for the story's sake. Although the writing may incidentally turn out to be another step in her recovery, that must not be her visible motivation: literary writing is not therapy. Her first allegiance must be to the telling of the story and I, as the reader, must feel that I'm in the hands of a competent writer who needs nothing from me except my attention.

I must feel confident that the writer is not using me to enhance her status or that of her family…with this "improved" version of her past. Bad Blood by Lorna Sage is one of the many examples of a memoir that avoids this pitfall.

I must also feel confident that I'm not being used by the writer to get revenge on one of the characters in the story…. On the other hand, anger, when it is perceived by the reader to be justified, need not be disguised or watered down.

Don't whine. Don't brag. Choose your targets carefully, sparingly, justly.

We're done here. More help can be obtained from the books by Barrington and by Brooks and Richardson (2012), among others.

WRITING A COOKBOOK

Don't take advice from me, a guy who rarely cooks. Instead, go to amazon.com and search for "how to write a cookbook," as I just did. Top of the list, with scads (=77, lots more than a dash) of enthusiastic reviews is…*Will Write for Food: The Complete Guide to Writing Cookbooks, Blogs, Reviews, Memoirs, and More, Second Edition,* by Dianne Jacob (2015). (What, no advice on writing menus? Next edition, please. Just kidding.) It sells for $10 for the Kindle and $14 for the paperback, and the reviewing culinary crew could not be more complimentary.

PERSUASION: *ETHOS, LOGOS, AND PATHOS*

Ethos, Logos, and *Pathos* are not Alexandre Dumas's *Three Musketeers* [Athos, Porthos, and Aramis], but rather the Greek for, approximately, character, logic, and emotion, three elements long identified as crucial for successful persuasive communication, important in our business and personal lives.

First, I must give credit where credit is due. I recently finished reading a fascinating and informative book: *The Power of Communication: Skills to Build Trust, Inspire Loyalty, and Lead Effectively,* by Helio Fred Garcia (2012), available in a Kindle ebook edition and hardcover through amazon.com. The lessons and examples are priceless, although I picked up the Kindle eb-ook for a song. I wish I could have read it when I was a debater in college eons ago.

To be persuasive, you must be credible. This is *ethos*. You must seem likely to know the topic you are addressing and to be committed to telling the truth about it. If you are attractive, in looks and personality, that helps. Dress appropriately. You seem likely to know the topic if you have the right credentials, including training, experience, and achievements. You seem likely to tell the truth if you have a history of honesty and no obvious reason to lie. If you are an interested, rather than disinterested party…if you will gain something by what you are "selling"… then you should admit that up front and hope that the power of your presentation will over-ride the tendency for your audience to doubt you.

Evidence and logic, the tools of rationality, help persuade others. "Logic" derives from *logos*. You can start from principles that your audience shares with you and proceed to show, by "deduction," that they support your case. Some people will find this highly persuasive. Another approach involves "induction," giving examples, evidence, leading to the conclusion you are offering. Often we try to do this with analogies, indicating that this is like that. The problem arises that no two situations are truly identical, so your audience may not find the comparisons compelling.

I have listed *pathos*, emotion, third because I am a retired scientist and I think that authority and reason should predominate, but psychologists tell us that emotional connection, empathy, must come first if we are to persuade others in daily life. We are ineffective if we approach them from "a mood apart." We need to "feel their pain" or seem to, "rejoice with them" if we can…. In his book, Garcia gives the example of the BP Chief Executive Officer Tony Hayward who, at the time of the major BP oil spill in the Gulf of Mexico from the oil rig *Deepwater Horizon*, said, "…there's no one who wants this thing over more than I do. You know, I'd like my life back." Hayward was widely criticized for seeming to be more concerned about his discomfort than the suffering of the Gulf Coast victims of that monumental oil spill. Here, displaying the wrong emotion doomed Hayward, and six weeks after this, he was removed from his CEO position.

To be persuasive, employ all three: *ethos,* be the kind of person who deserves to be believed; *logos,* present evidence and logic to justify your position; and most importantly, *pathos,* connect emotionally with your audience…be empathetic. You can do that, right?

HOW TO ORDER YOUR CHAPTERS

No, you cannot just call up the local fast-food emporium, the way you would to order take-out food. "Order" here means "sequence."

Imagine you have written nine chapters. What order shall you put them in?

If you are telling a story, as fiction or a memoir, you could tell it **chronologically**, a principle which dictates the chapter order. Often, this is not the most interesting arrangement, and you will likely start with a chapter that grabs attention, as well as sets the theme or a piece of the theme. That leaves you with the rest of the chapters to put in order.

You have more choices than you may be comfortable analyzing. Mathematics tells us that N chapters have N factorial = N! = (N)(N-1)…(1) possible orderings. For N=5 chapters this becomes 5!=5*4*3*2*1=120 possible orderings. N=9 chapters have 362,880 possible orderings. No wonder the choice can be difficult!

To simplify your problem, you need a method to your madness. Break the work up into major sections, then order within the sections. With N=9, three sections of 3 chapters each, the possibilities are 3!=6 orderings for each section, 6*6*6=216 for all the combinations of these when taken together, and 6 times this if the section orders are also free to be chosen, an improvement, a mere 1296 options. No wonder you need some principles to guide you, such as making the ordering in one section parallel that in another.

So, finding a principle on which to base the ordering is a plus for the writer, and for the reader, and breaking the work into sections simplifies the ordering choice even more.

HOW-TO BOOKS: STEP-BY-STEP

I checked Amazon today for books in the category "how to…." 655,335 entries came up. We know these books are popular and there are lots of them, including *How to Survive the End of the World as We Know it,* and the classic *How to Win Friends and Influence People.* **As our little secret, a potentially profitable writing niche, note that "how to build a gazebo" got only 23 hits.**

I went beyond Amazon: Googling "how to" got 3.48 billion results. As with so many such searches, I did not venture past the first page.

Knowing something about a topic and knowing how to do a particular thing within that general topic are very different. Understanding bicycles is not knowing how to ride one. I'm reminded of the joke told about one of my fellow physicists, who was said to know a hundred ways to make love to a woman, but he didn't know any women. I digress.

Let's go back to the example I gave near the beginning of the book and fill in that "how to..." outline:

What you are trying to do.

Your potential reader is likely to search for a book or article that starts with "how to..." and continues to name the particular goal. If you Google some topics, you will be amazed at the variety you find.

Here, I will show how to walk your dog, based on my interactions with our rescued Chow-Retriever, Colette. No, she is not "part Chow" because of her voracious appetite for only the choicest canned food. She is genetically part Chow and part Retriever, but fully "Daddy's girl," having me wrapped around her not-so-little paw.

Why it is important to you.

Try to think of all the reasons why doing this is important:

1. I'd rather walk the dog then clean up after her because I had failed to walk her.
2. I usually enjoy taking a bit of a walk, unless the weather is bad.

3. I know it makes Colette happy, because she makes a big fuss just before we go out.
4. She looks sad if I don't take her out.

Note the ordered, numbered list. People like lists. Specific, clear, finite, lists rule in the how-to genre.

Materials you'll need.

List what is needed and where to get it.

1. A dog. Call or capture yours. [See Figure 1, not shown here.]
2. A dog collar, attached to the dog.
3. A leash. Purchase one that is strong, hard to chew through. [Figure 2.] (On an early trek, our part-Chow chewed through hers.)
4. A little plastic bag to pick up feces. Buy at grocery store. [Figure 3.] (Carry this conspicuously, to reassure the neighbors, even if you don't always use it when you should.)
5. A dog treat, optional. (To reward good behavior, if it occurs and if it is observed. Note: praise is almost as effective and does not leave crumbs in your pocket.)
6. Clothing for dog walker, suitable for weather and neighborhood, and clothing for the dog, if you have that kind of dog.

Step-by-step instructions for accomplishing it.

1. Check the weather, by opening the door or window, or by listening to the radio or TV.

2. Call the dog. Example: "Come, Colette. Come, Colette. Colette, where are you?"
3. If calling fails, bring leash with you, attach it to dog's collar and gently lead the dog up to and out the door.
4. If calling succeeds, praise the dog ["Good dog, Colette!"], attach leash to dog's collar and gently lead the dog out the door.
5. If this is a "business trip," walk the dog where this will not cause angst in your neighborhood.
6. If necessary, remove excrement from ground and deposit in bag, praising dog for urinating or defecating outdoors rather than indoors.
7. Return home, walking as little extra or as much more as you deem appropriate.
8. Congratulate self and dog. Example, "Good dog, Colette."

What the outcome should be.

1. Dog will have done her "business."
2. You will have obtained exercise.
3. Floors indoors will not require supplementary cleaning.
4. Your "significant other," if there be one, will approve.

Sources of information and materials.

List them here, as appropriate. Numbered list, of course.

Surprisingly to me, how-to pamphlets and videos and books are big sellers, so go to it, providing somewhat more value to your readers than this brief example provided.

For extra value, and possibly extra money, produce a video.

HISTORY: FACTS AND INTERPRETATIONS

If you look to get instruction from me on how to write a history book, then history is not the genre for you. If you simply must write history, find some books specifically on the craft of writing history and books on the period of interest to you. A good friend, Dr. George Nash, is such a historian, having graduated *summa cum laude* from Amherst College and then obtaining a Ph.D. from Harvard University, where our friendship started.

To be taken seriously, you almost always need the skill, education, and credentials of such a scholar. **Consider writing about brain surgery instead, especially if you have had one, as two of my authors had.**

My role would come later, as an editor, something I did for a friend who was writing a book about a relative's espionage operations in the Civil War.

POLITICS: LEFT, RIGHT, MIDDLE, MUDDLE

Americans are strongly divided politically: some on the left, right, in the middle, and in a muddle. There's lots of interest in politics, and that interest will increase as we approach the presidential elections in 2016.

Feel free to write about your convictions, but know that your voice is likely to be drowned out by the multitude of experts, pollsters, commentators, editorialists, candidates, and past and present political advisers.

If you have celebrity or even renown, or if you have a reasonable hope of becoming known, then by all means write your

political polemic. Those who agree with you will tend to rate it favorably, and those who disagree will tend to disparage it. Perhaps some independents will be swayed.

I recall a study that showed the **same** material branded as either "Republican" or "Democrat" received higher or lower marks depending on whether the readers classified themselves as Republican or Democrat. "Where you stand often depends on where you sit."

As with much nonfiction, this genre will include a mix of facts and opinions, with, hopefully, some logical connections.

Although it has been said that we cannot each have our own set of facts, the truth is that **there is such a multitude of data comprising our world that, between what we select and what is pushed upon us by the sources we know and trust, we end up predominantly with the facts that support our preconceptions.**

I've watched the controversy over man-made global warming for the past many years. Being a retired scientist, as well as somewhat of a political junkie, and recognizing the cost and potential importance of controlling carbon emissions if they have to be controlled or enduring a significant change in the climate if that's what not controlling them would cause, I have been amazed by the ability of each side to cherry-pick the data so as to present plausible cases for and against stringent controls of fossil fuels in order to prevent anthropogenic global warming. Are we warming naturally, as we emerge from the Ice age of ten thousand years ago? Are we warming dangerously because of emissions of carbon dioxide and other gases? Are there feasible solutions? **Pick your expert, pick the periodicals**

and newspapers you typically read, pick your political party, and you've picked your answer.

To go from facts to conclusions, one needs logic. Sometimes fallacies are evident. Sometimes the technical analyses of the data, often statistical analyses, are baffling. Experts in the field will disagree on how much significance to give to small changes in measured quantities. Some will see the changes to be within the range of random variation, while others discern the troubling or reassuring trend.

Conclusions follow from facts and analysis, but even there we have to add another step in order to reach opinions: valuation.

Opinions are often based on values, rather than simply being the restatement of conclusions supported by facts. As anyone who has argued with someone from the opposing political philosophy knows, even agreement on facts and conclusions does not necessarily produce agreement on policies, because policies involve trade-offs, balancing values among competing parties.

One of my writing partners, Judith Axtell, whose *But…at What Cost* I edited, wrote of her gradual move from being rather traditionally liberal and Democrat to being rather solidly conservative and Republican, over the course of her 70+ years of life. She hoped that her example and her arguments would encourage those on her side and perhaps move some who disagree with her to reconsider their positions. She especially hoped that members of her own family would more clearly understand where she is now coming from. At the least, she got what she had to say "off her chest."

Another of my writer-coaching clients, Shaun Adkins of West Virginia, is finishing his *Squashing Liberalism,* with hopes of following the trail blazed by conservative stalwarts Rush Limbaugh, Ann Coulter, Mark Levin, Glenn Beck, *et al.* He already has gotten an Internet radio show, so he may be on his way to fame. Having published his book won't hurt.

PROFESSIONS: MEDICAL, LEGAL, TECHNICAL

If you are an M.D., D.D.S., O.D., P.A., or even an R.N., you are perceived by most people to have the credentials needed to write a book about a medical topic. For certain other topics, a law degree lends you credence, as do credentials like Ph.D., M.A., and M.S. Go to it.

If it is for fellow specialists, then you have a built-in audience. Do your best, as your competitors will be looking to show you up; your friends may give you some favorable reviews, though. For a wider set of readers, you will have to piggy-back on a current controversy or other newsworthy element.

I briefly helped a ghostwriter for a book on modern podiatry. The "author" enhanced his credentials. The ghost did the writing. I made a little money, too. Feet may have lost.

HEALTH: DIET, EXERCISE, MIND

Major categories for successful nonfiction books include health, wealth, and relationships.

Yes, we are all going to die sometime. However, we'd like it to be later rather than sooner, and along the way we would like to look good and feel good. So…diet and exercise, and maybe meditate.

If you have the credentials, possibly if you only have experience, you can write credibly about these topics.

One of my writer drop-outs wanted to write a book about weight loss through exercise and diet, having lost scads of weight she had put on during and after a divorce. **She took up body-building and developed a body that most men would like…to have themselves.** My limited test marketing with some women I knew indicated that they did not want to learn how to look like her.

I did learn that 3600 calories are equivalent to about a pound of fat, and that much of the early weight loss in various diets is due to excretion rather than fat loss. While most of us expend around 1500 calories per day, the Navy SEAL trainees expend 6000 calories per day.

If you want to look slimmer, you need to eat less and do more. Hey, I've got the basis for a book, *How to Look like a SEAL.* Maybe not. At least it isn't *How to Look Like a Seal,* although they are sleek.

Short of being a psychiatrist or a psychologist, what credentials do you need to be a mind- or mood-improver? One of my other writing dropouts was a kind of martial-artist-plus-meditator in a get-up, who eventually drifted off into multi-level marketing.

They say that old age is not for sissies, and neither is writing a book. Expect to spend hundreds of hours on it.

WEALTH: EARNING, SAVING, INVESTING

Do you want to write about money? Better have a lot of it. For credibility. Who heeds a pauper? Plus, to cover any lawsuit that might ensue from someone who followed your advice and failed. I'll say it here and perhaps elsewhere in this book: **take all financial advice, even or especially mine, with skepticism. Do your own "due diligence." "Past performance is no guarantee of future results."** Clear? Now we can continue.

Money! It makes "the world go around." Most people want to make more of it and waste less. For this genre, academic credentials seem almost irrelevant.

Having made a bundle brings credibility. Buffett, Gates, Trump, and their ilk are well suited to write, but often too busy getting richer. And yet, since "past performance is no guarantee of future results," as the SEC (Securities Exchange Commission) makes the investment community remind us all, we are to ignore (as if we could) that so-and-so got rich quick doing whatever it is he claims was key.

I can't imagine scientists saying "past performance is no guarantee of future results," or we'd have no science, no engineering, no equations, just hunches and guesses and a lot of bridges of doubtful reliability.

Saving is boring, but important. Putting a bit away regularly for a rainy day will enable you to buy an umbrella when you need one. If inflation kicks up, you may not be able to buy much more. **My favorite book in the wealth genre is _The Millionaire Next Door_ (Stanley, 2010), which shows how the old virtue**

of frugality retains its basic power: "Waste not, want not. Use it up, wear it out. Make do, or do without." Taleb's (2012) *Antifragile* would have you put a small but significant fraction into high-risk, high-payoff investments and the rest in the safest, stodgiest investments you can find. **You can double your money by playing red at roulette,** once, if successful. Hold back a little for bus fare for getting home.

Investing is like saving, only riskier. So many schemes, so little time, so little disposable income to put at risk. If you have a great idea, use it to make money rather than to sell a book. Typically, **once your great idea gets out, others will get into the act, and prices will be bid up or down to erase the temporary advantage.** If you are a Nobel laureate in economic theory, then you might establish a firm like Long-Term Capital Management, rely on exotic equations and naïve assumptions about probability distributions, and go belly-up impressively.

Writing a book about money should be approached with caution, because although "past performance is no guarantee of future results," you just might become rich and famous, which the tabloids demonstrate is no way to find happiness.

RELATIONSHIPS: FAMILY, FRIENDS, LOVERS, NEIGHBORS, COLLEAGUES

Oprah Winfrey has proven that you don't need a doctorate to be successful writing about, and talking about, relationships. Dr. Phil McGraw has shown that having a doctorate needn't get in the way.

These how-to books have the benefit of dramatic stories with often life-changing outcomes.

Clever titles help, like (Gray, 1992) *Men are from Mars and Women Are from Venus,* contrasting the god of war with the goddess of love. Hot tip: how about using *Men Are from Venus and Women Are from Mars,* contrasting guys with their heads in the clouds with women who like to vacation in places having canals? Obviously, no title should include Uranus.

The relationship book outline can resemble that of other how-to books:

1. The problem
2. Its significance
3. Your solution
4. Your products, services, programs, if any
5. Contact information

FICTION GENRES: AUDIENCE KNOWS WHAT IT LIKES

You wouldn't go to a movie without knowing the title of the film. If uncertain what the title implies, you would ask what kind of movie it is. Romantic? Comedy? Mystery? Drama? War? Horror? If you are not a fan of the movie's genre, you'll likely skip it.

Similarly, readers know what they want, and it is hard to get them to go far afield. Let's see: romantic, comedy, mystery, drama, war, horror…so far similar to the movies, but also paranormal, fantasy, historical romance, young adult, *etc.* Go to amazon.com and start to browse, and you will be presented with a smorgasbord of choices. [Metaphor, no food there actually.]

Evans (2015) classified novels' genres as follows: mysteries, science fiction, fantasy, Westerns, horror, thrillers, romance, historical. Another classification he offers depends on word count: adult commercial (80 to 90 thousand), science fiction and fantasy (100 to 115 thousand), middle grade (20 to 55 thousand), young adult (55 to 80 thousand), Westerns (50 to 80 thousand), memoirs (80 to 90 thousand)…though memoirs are not supposed to be fiction.

FICTION: TRUTH THROUGH FABLE—THEMES, SETTINGS, CHARACTERS, ACTION, DIALOGUE, DESCRIPTION, ARCS, FORESHADOWING, CLIFF-HANGERS, RESOLUTION

Note the Foreword to this book, which is Stephen King's Foreword to his own O*n Writing, Second Edition*. He's not sure anyone can tell another how to write outstanding fiction. Not having his skill and expertise, I will venture where he might not.

If you go to amazon.com and plunk down $11 for the Kindle ebook version or $14 for the paperback, you will likely profit from *Writing Fiction for Dummies* by Randy Ingermanson and Peter Economy (2009), which, when I looked, had received a couple of hundred very favorable reviews at Amazon. Naturally, the smart "Dummies" to whom the title refers are the would-be-author purchasers of this easy-to-follow handbook, rather than the audience for whom the writers of fiction will be writing… at least I hope so.

As I do not have the *Dummies* book myself, I'll lead off with advice from another source, which I do have. [A variation on the theme of "love the one you're with."]

Start with some good advice from novelist J.P. Kurzitza (2011) in a booklet *So You Want to Write a Novel:* "the story is everything. If you don't already have that, then this booklet won't be of much use to you." Without an engaging story, great language won't save you: "it's like spraying a skunk with perfume." [Notice that he avoids the over-used "lipstick on a pig" simile.] Later on in the booklet he offers three story templates to guide you. We'll look at two.

You've got to develop characters, plotlines, chapters, scenes for each chapter.

First, J.P. directs us to form a story "one sentence at a time," unearthing the sentences from our experience and information like an archaeologist would from a dig site. Start your dig with a mental picture of a scene and ask, **"What if...?"** When you have a good hypothetical, write it out as a sentence: "What if a cop is pulled over by another cop, harassing the first one who is working to expose police corruption?"

Characters must populate your story, characters we feel something about, we like or dislike, trust or distrust, *etc.* J.P. writes, "The focus for character development is to get personal with each character, even if they are minor characters."

Next, write the Prologue, but don't call it that, as many readers will skip it if you do. **Introduce the book with an important incident that makes the reader wonder**, "What the heck is going on here?" Make this incident crucial to the story. In my clearly nonfiction memoir, *Ting and I,* the opening chapter is "Home or Hospice," telling of the decision facing us when Tina emerged from 100 days in the critical care facility of our local hospital newly quadriplegic, dependent on a ventilator, fed and medicated through a gastric tube, given only a few months to live.

We next explore two of Kurzitza's "templates," fiction blueprints.

J.P. Kurzitza's "Template #1—Victories and Defeats"; his outline is:

- Introduction
- Major players in the story
- 1st minor victory for the protagonist
- 2nd conflict is encountered
- Revelation
- Start of the slow rise to the climax
- Welcome the supporting cast
- False optimism
- Relationships grow
- 3rd major conflict occurs
- 3rd major victory for protagonist
- Climax part I
- Climax part II
- Resolution
- Finish

Good plan, but you have to fill in the details! Introduce the major characters early and clearly described. Relationships develop. Conflicts arise. The protagonist succeeds in a minor way. The theme is revealed, what the hero must do and why and who or what stands in the way. A second minor victory is attained, but at a cost. Tasks and obstacles are encountered. Problems grow, however. Foreshadowing: little hints about the future warn the reader of trouble or suggest possible resolution.

Conflicts and resolutions follow, as the climax is approached. Unfortunately, a seemingly insurmountable problem arises, due to the antagonist. Our faith in the hero is shaken but not destroyed, and minor weaknesses in the antagonist's position become evident, soon to be exploited. Good triumphs, and the reader is satisfied.

J.P.'s "Template #2—Twists and Turns" has as its outline:

- Central theme of the story revealed
- Indisputable fact/truth revealed
- Protagonist's frailty revealed
- Introduction to antagonist_1
- Protagonist is introduced to antagonist_2
- Accidental revelation
- Plotline #1—main story mystery is discovered by protagonist
- Plotline #2—more trouble, secretly connected to Plotline #1
- Protagonist vs. antagonist_2
- Backstory to Plotline #1
- The trump card is discovered by the protagonist, little time left
- Protagonist's strategy changed or refined
- Backstory of the protagonist
- Epiphany, protagonist plays trump cost, at a cost
- Action
- Plotline #2 is explained
- Plotline #1 is explained
- Calm before the storm
- Between a rock and a hard place
- The rescue

- Primary climax
- End, resolution.

As Kurzitza (2011) notes. "Yes, the second template is quite complex and definitely worth a second or third read. But if done carefully and with great attention to detail, it can yield not only a thrill-a-minute story, but one that is very satisfying for the reader."

He offers an even more complex "Template #3," but you will need to get his book for it.

Let's address here some other aspects of the novel.

Themes: What is the point of your story? The unifying idea? You may even have some sub-themes.

Plot: Evans (2015) likes eight ways (the Chinese also think eight a lucky number) and presented "eight ways to develop your plot," to wit: 1. Have a **goal**. 2. The goal should entail **consequences**, gains and losses. 3. Mini-goals, **requirements**, must be satisfied along the way. 4. **Forewarnings,** events that suggest ultimate failure, should occur. 5. **Costs** must be paid in pursuing the goal. 6. **Rewards** will come, too. 7. **Prerequisites,** sub-goals, must be achieved. 8. **Preconditions,** plot complications caused by others, will intrude. **Finally, the protagonist clearly succeeds or clearly fails,** so the reader has the basic question resolved.

Settings: Your scenes occur at specific times and places. What are they? Describe them clearly and consistently.

Characters: Write up for yourself a dossier on each one, know each well and write some of what you know into the book as description or motivation. Evans (2015) gives eight ways to develop compelling characters: 1. **Introspection**, show them thinking to themselves. 2. Make them **opinionated**. 3. Put them at **risk**. 4. Set up a **love triangle** or similar competition. 5. Have them **behave differently in their group** than they might if alone. 6. Give them some **weaknesses if they are heroes** and some **virtues if they are villains**. 7. Give them **grudges,** scores to settle. 8. Have their **everyday interactions become unglued**.

Action: We get from one scene to another often through action. Events and actions create problems and opportunities.

Dialogue: The characters come alive in their interactions, including talking to each other. Dialogue can also give the backstory in bits and pieces, by allusions to events in the past. Conflicts develop and get resolved partly through speech. Word choice and diction can tell us about the intelligence, education, even some of the experience of the characters. If you have a good ear, and I don't, you can try to capture the particulars of dialect, but make sure your reader can understand what is being mumbled or said with a drawl or a brogue.

Arcs: An arc is a curve. A story with an arc will have a starting point, improvement or impairment, and an ending point. If it is U-shaped, the character will start high, hit a low, and eventually recover. For the inverted U, we have someone in trouble, rescued, only to fall back. Sometimes the arc will be wholly rising or wholly declining. It has been said that the problem with "middle-class tragedies" is that the hero has nowhere to fall from. **Over time, the protagonist or the situation or both must change.** Some element of returning has value. In Voltaire's

Candide, the "heroes" ("protagonists" in more formal terms), Candide and Dr. Pangloss, return after traveling far and enduring much and decide to [spoiler alert: do not read the rest of this sentence if you plan to read the novel] tend their own gardens.

It is said that there are four plots: hero pursues something, gets it or doesn't, is happy or unhappy with the result. That sounds too simplistic.

Foreshadowing: Generally this is a warning. If the enemy giant is approaching, you might first see his shadow. Time to run or get your slingshot. More broadly, foreshadowing gives the reader hints about what is to come so that it later seems plausible.

Cliff-hangers: When we last viewed the hero, at the end of a chapter, he was hanging from a cliff by a rope that was fraying. We'll get back to that, perhaps in the next chapter or the one after the next chapter, so keep reading.

Resolution: Unless you are writing a series of novels and are willing to risk the displeasure of your readers, at least some of the conflicts in your story line need to be resolved, the reader given a sense of satisfaction with how it all turned out. The reasons it turned out that way should seem plausible by the end.

Recall I noted the value of a strong opening chapter. Make the reader wonder about the outcome of something you get them to care about. Sketch the setting and main character, giving a little background information, but making clear the issue to be resolved. Present a conflict; later, resolve it.

Best-selling novelist Lee Child advises: **if you want to write a**

thriller, ask a question at the beginning and answer it at the
end.

HISTORICAL FICTION: BLASTS FROM THE PAST— ACCURATE SETTING, FICTIONAL PEOPLE AND DIALOGUE

**Historical fiction takes place in the past, which changes the
setting for the characters and their interactions. You still need
a strong story, but some of your readers will be reading partly
for the information about the times and the places in which
your characters are immersed.** They want to feel they are being
educated while they are being entertained. So, bone up on the
period and places in which your story unfolds.

The tricky part is not getting things wrong. The dialogue cannot contain modern slang and other anachronisms, items from
another period rather than the one you are dealing with. The
battles must be in the right places with the right winners. The
"news" of the time must be correct. Did they have indoor
plumbing? Radio? Electricity? Trains? You get the idea.

**Historical fiction seems to require less imagination and defi-
nitely more research than other genres,** but you cannot get so
bogged down in research that you stop writing the story. Readers
don't need all the historical details. Strike a balance.

As with other forms of fiction and for memoirs, **the writer needs
to make sure the reader knows the answers to the questions
journalists pose for themselves: Who? What? When? Where?
Why? How?** Similarly, the stories need to start with something
like headlines to alert the reader to what is coming: "The girls
never forgot that day…."

SCIENCE FICTION AND FANTASY: WHAT COULD BE, MAY BE—MAKE US CARE, MAKE US SCARED?

Googling "how to write science fiction and fantasy" produced 8 million hits. The winner: novelist Orson Scott Card's *How to Write Science Fiction and Fantasy,* the second print edition of which was published in 1991 and the Kindle ebook edition, which I bought for $5.75, published in 2015. It contains sound advice on his genres, followed by more about writing fiction in general. Here's material from Card's summary of the contents of his five chapters:

1. **The Infinite Boundary** *What is, and isn't, science fiction and fantasy....and how SF and fantasy differ from one another.*

2. **World Creation** *How to build, populate, and dramatize a credible, inviting world that readers will want to share with you....*

3. **Story Construction** *Finding a character for an idea or developing ideas for a character to enact.... Should the viewpoint character be the main character? ....The MICE quotient: milieu, idea, character, event....*

4. **Writing Well** *Keeping exposition in its place. Leading your reader into the strangeness, step by step. Piquing the reader's interest....*

5. **The Life and Business of Writing.**

Card (2001) tells would-be authors, "...in many ways this is the best audience in the world to write for. They're open-minded and intelligent. They want to think as well as dream. Above all, they want to be led into places that no one has ever visited before...."

So, get Orson Scott Card's ebook…it's a bargain.

ROMANTIC FICTION: LOVE LOST AND FOUND

On Writing Romance: How to Craft a Novel That Sells, by best-selling novelist Leigh Michaels (2007), is highly favorably reviewed on the amazon.com site, so who am I to disagree?

It will show you (the description says) how to:

- Steer clear of clichés
- Craft engaging and realistic heroes and heroines the readers will adore
- Convincingly develop the central couple's blossoming relationship
- Add conflict by utilizing essential secondary characters like "the other woman"
- Use tension and timing to make your love scenes sizzle with sensuality
- Get your characters to happily-ever-after with an ending your readers will remember forever.

This is not a genre with which I have much familiarity, despite being a romantic myself.

CHAPTER 3

PUBLISH

*Publishing a book is like stuffing a note into a bottle
and hurling it into the sea.*
Margaret Atwood, novelist, essayist, poet

The publishing industry has changed radically in the past few decades, due to the Internet and Print-on-Demand technology. Lower costs allow many more titles to be put up for sale, though they are then easily lost from view.

PUBLISHING'S LONG TAIL

"More nervous than a long-tailed cat in a room full of rocking chairs."

That simile need not describe the modern would-be book author. The publishing world has been changing, giving new-comers greater opportunities for being published, but making it less likely that their books will have large audiences. Let me explain:

Imagine creating the following graph: list the books published in the preceding year from 1 to whatever, in the order of their sales for that year, and plot the sales against that rank ordering. The best-selling book's sales would be plotted high, at position 1, the second-best-selling book's sales, somewhat less, at the number 2 and so on. The curve would fall continuously, but would go on and on, reaching values just somewhat larger than or equal to one book that year.

This kind of curve is said to have a "long tail," staying above zero much farther than most common mathematical curves would. There were several hundred thousand new titles published 2010, I have read, and the expectation for 2012 was a million or so, with the advent of electronic book publishing ("ebooks") and publishing on demand ("POD") printing technology. A decade ago, far fewer new titles were published.

Economics and technology enable this explosion in the number of titles "in print," where we consider those that are available as ebooks as being "in print," whether or not anyone prints them on paper.

My magnificent 2011 opus, *Ting and I: A Memoir of Love, Courage, and Devotion*, recently ranked about one-millionth on the Amazon list of printed published books sold by them and about 250,000th among their Kindle ebook offerings. Imagine if a book store was to try to keep the top million sellers, so you could be sure to find mine there: at a half-inch (1/24th of a foot) thickness average per book, and only one book on the shelf per title, the shelf space needed would be (1/24th) x (one million) x(feet) = 42,000 feet, almost eight miles of shelf space. [Mine would be way down at the far end.] I have read that a typical book store carries only about 25,000 titles.

No sensible book store would try to carry the top 1 million best sellers, and my *Ting and I* would be doomed. With the Internet and Amazon and my publisher's [Outskirts Press's] Print on Demand technology, my book has a chance to be seen on the Internet at amazon.com and bn.com *etc.* by people who would never have had that opportunity years ago.

This "long tail" situation allows economical production and electronic "storage" of far more books than ever before, giving the writer for a niche market a chance of being published and being read by his proper audience. The bestseller lists will rarely have such a title on them, but the book will be published, and its author will have a shot at reaching his intended readers. The costs for printing and storage will be relatively small, the profits per book possibly large, especially for ebooks, and the number of buyers largely dependent on the author's ability to promote himself and his work, as well as on the quality of the book itself.

Thus, this long tail can be to our advantage. We will be published. Next, we have to promote ourselves and publicize our book.

PRODUCE, PUBLISH, PUBLICIZE (SUMSION, 2010)

In her *Produce, Publish, Publicize,* author Sabrina Sumsion crisply covers these three aspects of becoming a successful author for **three different groups: the would-be bestsellers; the "make-a-buck" middle; and those who write for family, friends, and "posterity."** Available through amazon.com, her book looked good on my Kindle, and sold for a bargain price. This brief summary cannot do it justice. Buy it:

"Know thyself," Socrates reportedly said. If you think you can produce a best-selling novel or non-fiction book, then you are going to invest more effort in it than those who are writing it to send a message to the world or as an adjunct to their other activities or primarily to tell their story to their relatives.

Produce: Write the best book you can. Revise it repeatedly. Get help with editing for content and for copy correctness (grammar, spelling, punctuation). If you hope for a bestseller, you will have to pay for editing help, unless you land an agent and a contract with a traditional commercial publisher (those whose names you see on the spines of the best-selling books in your *genre*). Even then, you will likely need an editor to get your manuscript into tip-top shape for trying to snare an agent.

Publish: To get an agent, you will need to have high-class material and perhaps already be well known. Without an agent, forget about getting a traditional commercial publishing company to pay attention to what you submit. (Of course, rules have their exceptions, but although the race is not always to the swift, it pays to bet that way.) An agent will connect you with suitable publishing houses and should take your book on a commission basis only, typically 15%. (Avoid agents requiring up-front fees.) The publisher should give you a non-trivial advance and will supply editorial and art-work support and later will help with publicity. The middle category of authors will likely pay a few thousand dollars to get the book published by a subsidy press and will then hope to sell enough copies or give them away productively so as to offset the cost. If you are writing for posterity, you may be paying a subsidy press to publish your book and will probably be giving away almost all of your copies. Alternatively, you may use a service like Create Space to help you print and self-publish your book.

Publicize: There used to be hundreds of thousands of new titles sent forth in America each year. **The advent of easy self-publishing means a million or more new titles are newly minted yearly. How to get the public to buy yours?** The expensive way is to buy advertising. Harder, much less expensive, is to generate publicity. In bestsellerdom, the publishing house will do some advertising, will send you on some promotional trips, and will expect you to do what you can to get yourself and your book noticed.

Sumsion (2010) writes, "**Publicity is to books as wings are to birds.**" About half of her book is devoted to publicizing. **"Best-selling authors do not sit back and expect sales to come pouring in." They work very hard at promoting themselves and their work.** Publishers now expect this. A publicist herself, she recommends you hire one, but recognizes that this can be expensive and not truly necessary...if you have the skill and exert the effort to do what a publicist would do for you. She says you must not be discouraged by rejection: in a good week about 5 of 200 media contacts will result in a worthwhile interview, appearance, *etc.* She gives advice on finding a capable publicist. They will typically charge $1000 or more per month, and there are no guarantees, so don't mortgage the house to pay for one.

Getting noticed usually requires finding "the hook" for your book, something to catch and hold the media's attention. Sabrina **Sumsion lists twenty, including: current events; how to; top 10 (or any number); holiday (even create one); play on words; challenge; put the expert (me) to the test; connect to a celebrity; publicity stunt; involve the audience; involve the host; beware; discuss a problem; trends; make-over; controversy; success after failure; give yourself a special**

name (e.g., "the great____" or my sometimes title "the book obstetrician").

A professional publicity campaign starts with pre-publication publicity, where advance review copies of the book are sent to those who might be interested enough to read and comment on it, producing, hopefully, "blurbs" that can adorn the book's cover. You need press materials: "we consider a press release, a sell sheet, a Q&A, and two cover letters essential for a publicity campaign." See her book for details.

You'll want to send out free copies for reviewing once the book is published. Book signings where your book is on sale are good, but you can hold them at libraries, too. Book signings at book stores are becoming rarer.

The remainder of her book contains much valuable information on the details of getting favorable publicity.

PUBLISHING OPTIONS: TRADITIONAL, SUBSIDY, INDIE

Traditional publishing is done through a publishing house that will pay you an advance against the royalties that your book will earn. Because they are taking much of the financial risk, they are cautious about what writers they will publish. They will exert considerable authority over your manuscript's contents. It may be a year or two from submittal to printing. If they accept your book, they will print thousands, lowering their cost per page. They once did much book promotion, now less. Generally you will need an agent who will approach them and vouch for you and handle the subsequent negotiations. Getting an agent is usually hard, as they do not want to waste their time on someone whose book is not likely to sell well. They get a percentage of the royalties/advance. If you are a celebrity, they will even pursue you. If not, you take your chances with query letters and sample chapters. Many books are available on these topics.

Subsidy publishers, like Outskirts Press that I have used, will publish your book because you pay them to set it up, and they get some money from every copy sold. Although they want to keep their reputations intact, and thus won't publish just anything, they are much more likely to publish an unknown or a newcomer than are traditional publishers. They use Print on Demand technology and will print as few as five books at a time. You won't be stuck with a closet-full or a garage-full, but the cost will be around three cents per page. They will set up an author page for you, and they will offer a variety of editorial and promotional materials and activities for additional fees, but they will do minimal promotion for almost all their books.

Indie (independent) publishers will charge less than subsidy publishers and accept a wider range of materials, doing near-zero promotion. Depending on additional services, the costs are likely to be lower still than the other two options. Be sure to check, however.

CHAPTER 4

PROMOTE

Everyone lives by selling something.
Robert Louis Stevenson

By "promote," I'll be referring to the broader concept of marketing your book and yourself.

HOW TO GET MAXIMUM PUBLICITY IN MINIMUM TIME

Steve Harrison of Bradley Communications Corporation gave a web seminar, a webinar, having this title. I listened raptly as he presented over an hour of useful information for free, followed by a twenty-minute pitch for services his company offers.

Harrison started out in journalism, having majored in English in college. He soon joined his brother Bill Harrison in publishing the *Radio and TV Interview Report,* started in 1987, and the Harrisons and their Bradley Communications Corporation have by now coached over 12,000 authors and speakers, helping them to obtain successful promotion of their books and presentations.

The company's mission is simple: to help you achieve your mission. Among the successful authors that they have helped obtain widespread dissemination of their works are Jack Canfield and Mark Victor Hansen, whose *Chicken Soup...* line of books have sold over 500 million copies. Another author they helped to succeed is Dr. John Gray, whose *Men Are from Mars, Women Are from Venus* relationships book and associated activities have made him a millionaire many times over. They also coached Robert Kiyosaki, whose *Rich Dad, Poor Dad* book also rocketed into a highly successful worldwide publishing orbit.

Publicity is better than advertising because it is free, more credible, and tends to multiply, as media coverage leads to more media coverage. It's almost viral.

Publicity makes you an expert. This then increases traffic to your website, word-of-mouth recommendations, distribution, social media buzz, buyers for your product, and makes you sought out for speaking engagements and interviews, giving you the opportunity to raise your fees and product prices and generate even more publicity. You establish a virtuous circle, where success leads to more success. "The rich get richer." Well, less poor anyway, as most books lose money.

It surprised me to learn that **every day over 100,000 media outlets are seeking guests of one sort or another, interviewees who are in some sense experts, due to education, training, or experience.** Despite this, most authors and speakers fail to promote themselves successfully, remaining relatively unknown. Jack Canfield has commented that **not promoting one's book is much like giving birth to a baby and then leaving it on someone**

else's doorstep. If you have something worth communicating, then self-promotion also serves others.

Harrison described seven different ways in which famous authors and speakers differ from those who remain unknown.

First, the unknowns have tended to talk about their products, whereas the famous have understood that they must direct attention to good ideas. The famous understand the need for a "hook." A hook is an attention-grabber, a teaser, the kind of headline you see on the cover of popular magazines. On radio or TV a hook might be prefaced with the words "coming up...." What follows can usefully be a statement of how to do something, the countering of a myth, presentation of a prediction, or the proposing of a question, such as, "Is your house making you sick?" (I would add that journalists have a favored set of question starters: Who? What? When? Where? Why? How?)

Second, famous authors and speakers give reasons why they need to be covered NOW. They have a **timely** hook: a season, anniversary, holiday, news event—sudden or predictable.

Third, the famous authors and speakers have not relied on a single hook but have developed multiple, good hooks. Harrison gave as an example a hypothetical book, *Nutrition 101.* Certainly, one would approach media outlets that are centered on fitness and health, but Harrison gave examples of tailoring the message for those outlets interested in consumer affairs, personal finance, personal relationships, and self-improvement. An example from his talk would be for the author of *Nutrition 101* to offer to speak about "five ways to trim your grocery bill" or "how your beloved may be sabotaging your diet."

Speaking about multiple hooks, Harrison presented the following list of media interest groupings:

- Small business and entrepreneurial advice
- Parenting and family
- Personal finance
- Relationships
- Christian
- Women's
- Consumer advice
- Sales and marketing
- Psychology and self-improvement
- Health and fitness
- Leadership and management
- Career advice
- New Age and spiritual
- Alternative health.

No doubt there are more, and each of these could be further sub-divided into narrower niches.

Fourth, the famous utilize many different media types to maximize their exposure:

- Radio
- Television
- Newspapers
- Magazines
- Trade-published newsletters
- Blogs
- Podcasts
- E-zines

- Tele-seminars
- Webinars
- Conferences.

Who will become the new Oprah Winfrey? Bloggers may deserve this title. For example, the blog babble.com is the 276th most popular website, receiving over 4 million visitors per month. **To get your message on such a blog,** you can offer a guest post, offer to be interviewed, present a book to be reviewed, give away some chapters of your book, and offer your book as a prize. To be successful doing this, however, you must research the blog, to make sure that what you're offering is appropriate.

Fifth, the famous have had publicity plans, knowing WHO is their core audience, WHAT they read or watch, and WHEN various topics will seem timely to them.

Sixth, the famous often prepare the ground for their publications and presentations by getting publicity before the book is completed. One good way to do this is through the creation of short, few-minute videos, placed on YouTube, which has become one of the top search engines on the Internet. In 3 minutes one might cover a topic such as listing "the top reasons men are afraid of commitment." Be sure to include links to Facebook, Twitter, and LinkedIn.

Seventh, the successful have learned that they cannot do this all on their own. There is a lot of work involved, with special skills, data bases, and experience needed. They need the help of professionals, such as the Harrisons and their Bradley Communications Corporation. For $2500, the Harrison's will give you an in-depth consultation with one of their consultants, at least four valuable publicity hooks, three half-page ads in their *Radio and TV Interview Report*, four ads in their publication *Experts4Interviews*, a 90% discount on attending Steve Harrison's multiple-day $2000 publicity workshop, and they will shoot, edit, and upload five videos for you. They placed the value of this package at over $5000. Those who are interested in learning more about their program should go to the website http://specialpublicityoffer.com .

UNSELFISH SELF-PROMOTION (OLSON, 2009)

The Internet provides unprecedented opportunities for Jorge Olson's Three Cs: Communicate, Collaborate, Commercialize. Get known, liked, trusted. Form partnerships. Give value for value.

The key: **be generous**, unselfish in your self-promotion, as Olson (2009) writes:

…the notion of promoting yourself by being unselfish is very powerful, and you will be an expert by the time you are done reading this book…. Being unselfish is nothing new in business or politics, especially among seasoned salespeople. In sales, you place the customer first. This is an example of unselfish promotion.

To help others, you have to understand their needs and wants. They will then appreciate what you do for them, because what you choose to do will be suitable, appropriate to their wants and needs. Unlike most people, you will be spending somewhat less time thinking about yourself and somewhat more time thinking about them.

By writing, you establish a link, a connection with people that lasts at least as long as it takes them to read what you have written, and which may stay in their minds much longer. You have usually given them something of value, which may make them want to reciprocate.

Writing helps you add to your promotional toolbox, which includes Internet marketing, articles, social networking, public speaking, business cards (some people use several different types), books, press releases, videos, webinars....

The key is that you give before you get.

For business owners, Olson (2009) posits Internet Marketing Rule #1: Don't build a self-indulgent website. Writers can profitably heed this, as well: promote your book or books on your website, but give the visitors something more: excerpts, deals, related information on the books' topics, colorful and interesting graphics, information about writing or the book industry. Give value to get eyeballs.

Olson's Internet Marketing Rule #2: Build value: "you have to provide what people look for, information, entertainment, collaboration, or commerce." Build the website for the visitors' benefit. They say, "Content is king." Valuable content, that is.

As an author, you will likely have an author website, which is your main website, and websites for each of the books you have written. Give stuff away. Collect email addresses. Make sure they know how to reach you.

For more details on unselfish self-promotion see Olson (2009).

AUTHOR SUCCESS GUIDE (BAREHAM, 2013)

Steve Bareham, the author of *eBook author success guide—1:*

Self Publishing eBooks, lists not 4 Ps or 5 Ps for success, but 12 Ps:

- **Product:** What are you offering? What is it worth?
- **Proof:** Be sure you are better than your competitors in meeting readers' needs.
- **People:** Who wants or needs your book? What are they like?
- **Perception:** How attractive are your book, your ads, and your writing?
- **Position:** What is your USP, your Unique Selling Proposition? What's "best" about it?
- **Price:** Bareham believes the $0.99 ebook is on the way out. Amazon favors $2.99-$9.99, and the market is willing to pay more for "how-to" books than for other types.
- **Problems & Pitfalls:** Try to predict and avoid them!
- **Promotion:** "…pretty much everything that you do to boost sales: your website, your blog, participation by you and others in reader forums, reader reviews, advertising, video, etc…."
- **Pro-active follow-up**: Get opinions from your readers.
- **Place:** Where your books can be found, obtained.
- **Processes:** Ease of purchase, guarantees, etc.
- **Persuasion:** *Ethos, pathos,* and *logos*…credibility, emotion, logic.

Bareham (2012) has separate sections in his guide on using the following to promote your books:

- YouTube videos
- Website
- Weblog (blog)
- Sample chapters given away
- Audio book format
- Social networks
- Book reviewers

Near the beginning of his *eBook author success guide,* he admonishes us to:

- Keep writing, as the more books you publish, the better known you become and the more your books will sell.
- Keep promoting yourself and your books.
- Solicit 5-star reviews from likely providers.
- "Understand viral leveraging."
- Use apt "tags" on your Amazon book descriptions.
- Avoid a book title that is too cute. [It can get lost among Amazon's 10 million, he warns.]
- Consider the substantial advantages of Amazon's Kindle Direct Publishing.
- Get to know and use GoodReads.

THE AUDIENCE REVOLUTION (INY, 2015)

You have written your book, gotten it published, obtained some favorable reviews, given a few talks here and there, and gotten some press. Despite that, you have sold a hundred or fewer copies, just like the overwhelming majority of non-celebrity, first-time authors.

Where did you go wrong? Like me, you thought, *build it and they will come,* write it and they will buy it. As recently successful author, program developer, marketer Danny Iny of Firepole Marketing explains: one must build one's audience first.

Makes sense, actually. Celebrities have successful memoirs because they already have big audiences, and unless the book is a dud, they are going to sell myriads, or at least a whole lot.

Iny's book is *THE AUDIENCE REVOLUTION: The Smarter Way to Build a Business, Make a Difference, and Change the World.* It lives up to its title. Well, maybe "change the world" is a bit premature.

Iny has a great line: **"failure is only failure if it happens in the last chapter. Otherwise, it's a plot twist."** This 2015 Easter morning, minister Joel Osteen spoke about one of the messages of Easter: it's not over just because it seems to be a failure; something better beckons. A sage is said to have remarked, when asked what is universally true, "This, too, will pass." We must persevere.

Those of us who have not yet built an audience can still do so. In the next chapter of our lives, we should take Iny's advice: examine our passions, find what others have asked of us already, and look for the intersection of these that marks our best choice for making a contribution others will value.

Iny's book offers a link for a site with a video and worksheets to help in this exploration.

PROMOTING YOUR BOOK AND YOURSELF: KNOWN, LIKED, TRUSTED...K, L, T

Public relations experts often refer to "K, L, T," meaning "known, liked, trusted," the progression of confidence that people have with someone who starts out as a stranger to them, whom they come to know and like and trust to the point of being willing to buy something from them.

MARKETING YOUR BOOK

You have written your book and now have to get someone to read it, and better yet, get many people to buy it. That was the problem I was faced with. If you are a memoir writer, you have the advantage of a fairly popular *genre* and the disadvantage of having only one memoir and not a series of memoirs that might support each other. If someone likes your memoir, you do not have another to offer.

Early in my quest for book marketing insight, I found John Locke's (2011) *How I Sold 1 Million Ebooks in 5 Months!* His ebooks were novels, sold at $0.99 each, nine different titles, five with the same "hero," the somewhat unsavory Donovan Creed. Locke sold this How-To book for $4.99, correctly predicting that would-be self-publishing authors, such as myself, would readily ante up the big bucks for it. Glad I am that I did. Well, pretty glad.

I will paraphrase Locke's "Business Plan" and compare it with my own efforts for my book:

1. Write the best book you can. Done: *Ting and I: A Memoir.*

2. Create a website. Done: tingandi.com .
3. Use Twitter to get people to your website. Done: "@doug-laswcooper" has approximately 10,000 "Followers."
4. Answer all your emails from readers. Will do.
5. Create a simple blog site. Done: http://douglaswin-slowcooper.blogspot.com. By June 2015, I had posted over 400 blog entries in a four-year period. They averaged about 100 visits per entry. Not a big deal, but not chopped liver, as they say in New York City.
6. Use Twitter to call attention to your blog. Doing it. Facebook, too.
7. Epublish your ebook. Done, through Outskirts Press and as Kindle book through Amazon.
8. Repeat the cycle with other books you write. Doing it.

Locke maintains that his low ebook price, $0.99, encourages uncertain buyers to try his novels, as it did me. He by-passed conventional publishing houses because he wanted to write his books his way, not theirs. **He tried many of the suggestions offered him for marketing, but eventually came down to his website—blog—Twitter Internet triad for success.** He emphasized, as well, that he wrote his books with a particular kind of reader in mind, his market niche. Depending on the kind of life you have led, you may have significant constraints on niche-seeking. **Some of Locke's luster lessened when it was found that he had paid for many of the favorable reviews that helped propel his books high on the bestseller lists.**

Amanda Hocking, twenty-something author of "young-adult paranormal" novels [*USA Today*, February 9, 2011] sold 450,000 ebook copies of her nine titles, most priced at $0.99, in January of 2011 alone. She writes about vampires, zombies *et al.*, and promotes her book through a blog, Twitter and Facebook. Social media move ebooks as well as helping to sell conventionally published works.

Back to Locke, who emphasizes writing for one's target audience, finding them, interacting with them, listening to them. With a memoir, perhaps your audience is People Like You. There are elements of our story *Ting and I* that should have had wide appeal to:

1. Women who like romance stories.
2. Would-be career women whose marriages had to come first.
3. Asian-American women, especially those of Chinese ancestry.
4. Couples in their second marriages, with step-children.
5. Couples with one member seriously handicapped or critically ill.
6. Nurses, doctors, social workers who deal with the critically ill.
7. Families providing prolonged health care at home.
8. Those making decisions about hospice care.
9. All who like inspirational stories about a person's success against the odds.

Your book will have a different niche, or niches, but as you identify them, they should suggest key words to use in Internet searches to find the magazines and ezines that your potential audience reads. We were able to get some articles that mentioned our memoir published in magazines and ezines that served these niches.

Both the United States' and Britain's national multiple sclerosis (MS) societies accepted articles about us and our book, "Undefeated" and "A Book for My M.S. Heroine," as Tina's quadriplegia is due to M.S. The online monthly publication, asiancemagazine,com, for Asian American women, has accepted each article I submitted monthly for the past fifty months. Youandmemagazine.com accepted three pieces, as they are interested in first-person articles dealing with aspects of medicine. Wellspouse.com accepted "Interracial Stepparent and Caregiver." *Marriage Magazine* accepted "Together Forever." I have been less successful in getting pieces in publications for seniors or into any of the general-circulation magazines, such as *Women's Day,* which magazines tend to limit their acceptances to writers with established national reputations and clippings.

Joining the Orange County [NY] Chamber of Commerce opened up many useful channels. I have written several pieces that were published in their monthly public newsletter [circulation 80.000], gotten excellent advice on marketing and help in doing it from fellow members, and have enjoyed involvement with a nice group of people, thus alleviating some feelings of isolation. The Chamber members I talked with encouraged me to start a blog, a personal web site that contains samples of my writing and allows others to comment on them. A member gave me valuable advice on improving our web site and others are planning to go well beyond that in improving my visibility in social media.

Concerning advice he received from others, **John Locke noted** that the following ***did not work out*** for him:

1. **Trying to get his books into bookstores** [need an agent and a publisher].

2. **Trying to get interviewed by newspapers.** [We did get a very nice interview article in a local weekly paper and an exceptionally sympathetic and well-received article in a local monthly magazine.]
3. **Hiring a publicist.**
4. **Sending out press releases.**
5. **Radio interviews.**
6. **Paid advertising in various media.**

Locke welcomes the rest of us to try our luck, but his explanations of his experience made sense to me, so I did very little of the above.

Where does that leave us? Good book, web site, blog, Twitter, and prayer.

P.S. In 2015, after four years of my promoting my *Ting and I,* I was given the gift of an hour with a professional book publicist from the Bradley Communications group. We discussed what I had done to promote the memoir, and he told me I had done the right things and that memoirs from unknown people rarely do even as well as the few hundred I had sold.

TWEETING ON TWITTER

Twitter lets you reach a wide audience with a short message, 140 characters of less, a Tweet. On Twitter I've been twitter. com/douglaswcooper, aka @DouglasWCooper] since June 2009, I have Tweeted 25,000 Tweets and acquired nearly 10,000 Followers, people who have agreed to let my Tweets pass through their Home page. On the average, my Tweets are seen by about 100 people each time. About 1% to 2% of each time, someone will respond, such as clicking on a link, Retweeting to others' Followers, being Favorited, or inducing someone to go from my Tweet to my Profile page, where they see a very short biography that mentions my Ph.D., my memoir, *Ting and I*, as well as my coaching, and shows the link to writeyourbookwithme.com.

As they pass through others' Home pages, Tweets have a short lifetime, one estimate being eight minutes. About 10% of my Followers are on Twitter during any hour, thus an audience now of 1000, so getting 100 of them to see the Tweet isn't bad, the rather common 1% response rate out of the 10,000 person base.

Without celebrity, how did I build up to 10,000 Followers? My advice:

1. **Follow lots of people and organization** whose Tweets you find interesting. The big fellas won't Follow back, but they give you Tweets worth Retweeting, which will attract others to Follow you.
2. **Favorite** interesting stuff, especially from those you want to befriend. It's pleasant, positive, and appreciated.
3. **Follow** all who Follow you, except those who are selling Followers on Twitter, useless stuff, pushed by people who Follow you briefly then are dropped by Twitter or who drop you.
4. **Almost never criticize** others on Twitter.
5. **Retweet** links to interesting material.
6. **Keep your promotion of your own stuff to 10% or less of your Tweets.**
7. **Be active with the people with similar interests**, indicated by hashtags, such as #promocave for writers and

#tcot for conservatives on Twitter, for me. Retweet and Favorite their material, and they will do so for you, spreading it to a wider audience.

8. **#promocave in particular, run by @JorgeOlson,** started with a campaign to get writers to Follow each other, and moved on to promoting books and sharing writing advice. It seems to be a labor of love for Olson, although promocave.com is an affiliate marketer for Amazon, and books that are bought by clicking through from promocave.com earn the site some money. **I don't do affiliate marketing, as I don't want to seem to have a conflict of interest, perhaps recommending books only to get paid.**

I don't know how many visits to tingandi.com were induced by Tweets of mine, and I certainly don't know if I sold any books that way, but I did get one valuable writing partner through Twitter and one bogus potential client from Nigeria, whose name I keep on my personal list of clients...to keep me humble.

BLOGGING ALONG

In mid-2011 as I was finishing *Ting and I,* I started a WordPress blog, douglaswinslowcooper.blogspot.com, to gain another outlet for free promotion of me and my stuff. **I serialized my memoir on the blog, right after it was published**, gaining it another 100 for-free readers in a typical week, and since it was written as a message book rather than a commercial book, I was pleased.

I posted material I wrote for the Orange County Chamber of Commerce and some local businesses and posted articles that were later published elsewhere.

Once I started getting writing clients, I got the permission of some of them to serialize their books after they were published, giving them and me a boost. In one case, I serialized only the odd-numbered chapters, at the co-author's request.

I blogged articles of mine on writing, many of which are the backbone of this book, and when I wanted to recruit more clients, taking the advice of my marketing adviser from SCORE, Edison Guzman, I blogged "Why Would a Former Harvard Professor Want to Help You Write Your Book for $25 per Week?" and "7 Questions Answered about Writing and Publishing with a Book Coach." I also wrote "The Subjunctive Mood" and "—ing: Participle or Gerund" and put some of my 60-odd reviews written for Amazon on the blog. These posts each averaged a hundred views.

I pointed people to my coaching blogs via Facebook, and the coaching blogs themselves had a video of me and had the writeyourbookwithme.com link and a "Call to Action" to go to that page. A couple of my new clients, at least, can be credited to the blog-website combo. And I had fun writing and posting.

The exposure was "free," unless you considered what my time was worth in doing it.

ADVERTISING ON SOCIAL MEDIA (GUZMAN, 2015)

Public relations management and book promotion are essentially ways to get free advertising. If you are making a few dollars per book or less, you need to be frugal. I spent almost nothing on advertising *Ting and I*. What I did do was promote it on its own website, tingandi.com, and on Twitter and through my blog, by serializing it, as described above.

As a benchmark comparison, we'll price Social Media (Facebook) advertising against local classified ads. My paid advertising has been almost exclusively for my coaching program, Write Your Book with Me, as each person who enrolls will spend about $1000 on my coaching and editing, taking roughly a year. Over the past few years, I have run a weekly classified ad in our small local paper, *The Wallkill Valley Times*, at the modest cost of $5 per week:

WRITE AND PUBLISH YOUR BOOK
With my help. Douglas Winslow Cooper, Ph.D.
845-778-4204. douglas@tingandi.com

or

TELL YOUR STORY. WRITE YOUR BOOK
With my help. Douglas Winslow Cooper, Ph.D.
845-778-4204. douglas@tingandi.com

I got about one client per year from these ads, at the cost of $250/year. Perhaps I picked up some goodwill from the editor as well, as the paper ran a few stories about me and my authors.

Accommodating myself slowly to the twenty-first century, I sought and received some valuable free consulting from SCORE advisor Edison Guzman, head of A E Advertising (aeadvertising.com). As I described in a testimonial I wrote for SCORE and Edison [reciprocity, one hand washing the other]:

"...and Guzman SCOREs!" If small business had a play-by-play announcer, that would have been his exclamation, commenting on the help SCORE's Edison Guzman has given me. Edison's seminars and counseling sessions have provided me the most value I've received from my membership in the Orange County Chamber of Commerce, and I have gotten a lot from being a member.

Edison got my attention this April with his day-long free SCORE seminar, *"Social Media Marketing Strategies for Small Business Owners,"* although I had already known, liked, and been impressed by him during my four years in the Chamber. **Not only did the seminar awaken me to useful Facebook strategies, I found I was eligible and welcome to obtain free business counseling through SCORE at the Chamber. Who knew? Sign me up!**

I really needed Edison's help with advertising, in particular on Social Media, like Facebook, Twitter, and my blog. His first counseling session started with a discussion of my goals: **I help people write and publish their books—as a coach, editor, even co-author—and I wanted another half-dozen clients this year.**

Next came his exploratory question, *"What is your unique value proposition? What sets you apart? Tell me about yourself and your business."* As we talked, Edison grew even more enthusiastic. **He quickly nailed it, a theme for me: "Why would a former Harvard professor want to help you write your book for only $25 per week?"** That became the basis of the Social Media campaign: on my blog, on Twitter, on Facebook. In subsequent sessions, he then showed me in detail how to use these tools successfully to recruit my next set of would-be authors.

The difference between a lecture and an expert's hands-on consulting, which is what our SCORE sessions became, is the difference between learning a bit about something and actually knowing how to do it. I knew I wanted to advertise on Facebook as well as use its free features, but I needed help in negotiating the various set-up pages, in choosing my target market, my message, the optimal mode of delivering it, and even the best titles for my ads. Edison helped me by a combination of "fishing" for me and "teaching me how to fish," so I could do it myself soon after. *So many options existed, and Edison explained each of them to help me make good decisions.*

Discouragement can come easily to the small businessman. Actually, I am of medium size, but my business is small, and I don't always persevere. *Without Edison's guidance, I might have given up on advertising on Facebook,* thinking the cost per response my ads were getting to be too expensive, but he reassured me that my Facebook ads were doing very well. We tweaked them, and they did even better.

Edison, drawing on his advertising expertise, taught me some of the factors that help motivate potential buyers to close the deal rather than procrastinate. We developed a campaign that reached potential clients with attractive messages about becoming authors [they are authoritative] or memoirists [they preserve memories], emphasizing the limited number of candidates to be accepted [six] in the limited two-week enrollment period. *All along, we've had fun, as I have been learning so many things I had not been taught as a physics major.*

I am looking forward to continuing to access Edison's valuable expertise. *The Social Media campaign he helped me with has already brought me half my quota of new clients, and the enrollment period has not yet begun.*

I'd say, we SCOREd!

As the testimonial attests, I am high on advertising professional Edison Guzman and his help. I attended his day-long seminar "Facebook Marketing for the Small Business Owner." [He tells me that these seminars net him 10-20% of the attendees as clients, even though he does no self-promotion during them.]

In April 2015, there were over 1.4 billion Facebook users. Almost 900 million of them log in daily. Let's see: if I got only 1% of them, I would have 9 million clients. That seems optimistic. However, he reported that 42% of marketers report that Facebook is critical or important to their business. Who am I to argue with that?

There are many ways to reach people via Facebook: Timeline, Like, Share, Chat, Comment, Photos, Video, Tags, Groups, Lists, Pages, Events, Subscribe, and Advertise. Edison focused on advertising, which has its own Facebook sub-specialties: buying ads for the Newsfeed or the Right-Hand Column, or for Mobile viewing; Boosting a Post, getting others to Like your page, etc.

Edison Guzman advised me that before we start an Ad Campaign, we recognize that our efforts to get others to know, like, and trust [K, L, T] should reflect an awareness that people are not on Facebook to be sold stuff, but to connect with others and be entertained and informed. His five crucial ingredients to advertising on Facebook:

1. **You must create a Page specific to your audience.** [I set up Douglas Winslow Cooper with a link to my web site writeyourbookwithme.com.]
2. **You must target your audience with laser-like precision.** [Tricky, as a discussion of my subsequent efforts will reveal. I did figure my would-be memoirists would likely be women over 50 and my businessmen would be men over 50.]
3. **You must have attention-grabbing images.** [As a writer, I naively put much more emphasis on words rather than pictures. Make sure you have free images or pay the producer, or you can get sued,]
4. **You must use logical headlines appropriate to your reader.** [See below, I thought to reach adults generally with "Tell your story," memoirists with "Memoirs preserve memories," and business folk with "Authors are authorities."
5. **You must have an appropriate Call to Action.** [What's that? Click here to...go to my web site, go to my blog site, go to my book site, Like my Page, *etc.*]

Edison next discussed how to target your audience. Some of this targeting is by demographics: geographical location, age, gender. Facebook also has information on their interests, the categories and hashtags they like, their friends and Likes and groups and .... Presumably the FBI has somewhat more information, but Facebook may be close.

To advertise on Facebook, get to know their rules, especially their taboos.

I already had a blog and a LinkedIn account and a Facebook

page with a business page having 50 Likes. I had nearly 10,000 "Followers" on Twitter, about half of whom Followed me when I started as a political Tweeter primarily, and the other half of whom Followed me in my reincarnation as a writer-coach-editor.

I knew nothing about advertising on Facebook, and this became my first priority. **Edison showed me how to set up a simple ad. First, we get attention with a headline:** "Tell your story." "Authors are authorities." "Memoirs preserve memories." **Then we follow with a short description**, such as "Write your book with a professional book coach." **Don't forget your Unique Selling Proposition and your Call to Action.**

Although I got to it later rather than sooner, running a "Like" campaign on Facebook is a good idea, because you can then target those who Liked you with your ads. [No good deed goes unpunished.] Essentially, post stuff on your Page that your target audience will Like, then let Facebook seek out people in the categories you choose to induce them to Like it, using your ad and a Call to Action of "Click on Like." Well-performing ads will cost about $0.01/person reached and about $0.50-$1.00 per person who Likes the site.

Edison directed me to Create Ads on Facebook. What I wanted to do was get people to go to my "lucrative" coaching writeyourbookwithme.com site, rather than my message memoir site, as I make less than a dollar per book from selling *Ting and I.* First, I ran a week of ads which targeted men and women in the U.S. I chose the lowest cost, $5/day. The goal was to get the readers to click on writeyourbookwithme.com. The metrics we followed were cost/reach, usually around a penny a person who saw the ad, and cost/click, which ranged from a half dollar to a few dollars per person who clicked on the link to my website.

Ideally we wanted people who clicked on the site to then fill out our contact form, getting their email address and their expression of interest in writing a book. I tried male only and then female only, with different pictures for each, and used "writing" as an interest. I stuck with targeting people over 50 years of age. I got much the same results with highly local ads as with all-U.S. ads. **A Facebook staffer wrote me not to worry too much about optimizing demographic parameters. I learned elsewhere that Facebook does some dynamic adjusting of the targeting as the ad period continues,** so understanding exactly what worked and what didn't is obscured with this "black box," while it does improve performance.

As it has turned out, most options tried gave us reach at a $0.01/person, with 1% to 2% clicking the site at about, thus $0.50-$1.00 per click. Spending $400 obtained about 4 new coaching clients, thus a cost of $100 per client. "About 4" indicates that how and why they found me was not always clear.

To put it into perspective, my classified ads cost me about twice per writing client as did my Facebook ads. My book site, tingandi.com, cost me only about $100 over four years, has had about 4000 hits, and I have no way to know how many books it sold, but it had to be at most 200.

I viewed the advertising expense as partly an educational expense. Facebook let me see how many potential ad viewers I had for a variety of demographic, geographic and interest parameters. I experimented with different photos [supplied by

Facebook] and even different wording. The experiments had to be set up carefully so that only one variable was changed as we went from one ad to the next.

Edison taught me how to add a sense of urgency to the campaigns and how to develop attention-grabbing headlines. I also found on the Internet useful information and tools for generating effective titles and headlines (headlinerr.com).

I concluded that for high-value enterprises like coaching and consulting, Social Media advertising is worthwhile. For indie authors with books to sell, the price is likely too steep. Your experience may be quite different, and "past performance is no guarantee of future results."

GOING VIRAL (ADAMS, 2013)

A virus, such as the flu, spreads rapidly as each person infects a few others, so 1 infected becomes 2, and 2 become 4, and by the tenth infection period 1000 are sick, and by the 20th period, 1 million are. Without making anyone sick, **you want your book to spread like the flu. To do so, you need many enthusiasts and few nay-sayers.**

In his ebook *Viral: How to Spread your Ideas like a Virus,* R. L Adams (2013), much as an epidemiologist would, describes spreading your book virally, in his chapters covering:

- **The Viral Factor:** Adams starts with a telling quotation from Robert Stephens, with whom I am not familiar, **"Advertising is a tax for having an unremarkable product."** If it's wonderful, the world will catch on. A bit

harsh, but with a grain of truth, especially now that we have the Internet and Google *et al.* Since we are all connected, we can hardly help catching the fever of the latest fad, or, better yet, of your book. Transmission can be fast and wide. Typhoid Mary was a piker. Unfortunately, we are awash in new stuff, some good, some not. You want to stand out by providing value uniquely, to others. You hope to reach Malcolm Gladwell's (2006) "tipping point," where success feeds on success exponentially. Simplicity helps. **Real viruses are simple, too. So... unique, useful, uncomplicated: U, U, U.**

- **The Virus:** It can be an idea that spreads rapidly, or a video, a picture, a movie, a book, a product...the unique, useful, and uncomplicated spreads if transmission is easy, as with YouTube videos. **The unique, useful, uncomplicated becomes ubiquitous. U,U,U,U. It has "gone viral."** Popularity breeds more popularity, celebrity more celebrity. It "feeds on itself" like a nuclear chain-reaction. Think of Google, Facebook, Twitter, sudden-hit singer Susan Boyle....

- **The Message: "In business it's a professional marketer's job to tell us stories.** These stories are at the very heart of their advertising campaigns." Adams cites Christopher Booker's *Seven Basic Plots:* **1. Insurmountable Obstacle**...e.g., David vs. Goliath, Apple vs. IBM. **2. New Beginnings**...a rebirth of a company once in decline. **3. Rags to Riches**... *Cinderella,* Dell Computers. **4. Comedy**...the unexpected, the GEICO Gecko. **5. Tragedy**...if only Romeo and Juliet had had cell phones! **6. A Quest**...*Don Quixote,* the Lexus quest for perfection. **7. Transformation through Travel**...*The Wizard of Oz, Candide.* A successful virus will tap into strong emotions, as the Marlboro Man tapped into the inner yearning of many men and the admiration of many women.

- **The Transmitter: We share information we have obtained from trusted sources,** often people we know personally or have come to know through the media. Sharing creates the viral spread. **Unique, useful, and uncomplicated still are required for ubiquity. Entertaining beats boring.** Transmitters with large audiences whom they engage often will spread ideas most rapidly, using conventional and Internet Social Media. Check out their Klout scores on Klout.com. A few Power Users of Social Media outweigh a multitude of "nobodies." If you can stomach it and can arrange it, strategically "befriending" a Power User before pushing out your idea pays off handsomely. No bribing, however.

- **The Capsules: You can provide a giveaway, but target it carefully** and limit it to what you can afford. A clever photo plus caption may go viral. A service, like Facebook or Hotmail, can go viral. Movies and books rarely do so, *Harry Potter* being an exception. "The Internet…is enamored with video." Recall Susan Boyle and her *Britain's Got Talent* appearance video or singer Psy's Gangnam Style videos that received a billion viewings.

- **The Environment:** Adams quotes marketing and management guru **Peter Drucker, "The aim of marketing is to make selling superfluous."** The customer is, effectively, pre-sold on the product or service. Just as the flu transmits more readily in the fall, your virus will do better or worse depending on environmental conditions. What's trendy? Piggy-back. "Find the customers, then create your idea….Spot a void then fill it….come up with a story…."

- **The Transmission: Live by word-of-mouth, die by word-of-mouth.** Unique, useful, uncomplicated help adoption and spread, especially if easily transmitted. What do your customers want? An ex-Google guy, Clark Williams, and his friend Jack Dorsey started Odeo, which, on the verge of failure, was mutated to become Twitter, a big success partly due to its ease of transmission. Monitor transmission with Google Analytics and Facebook Analytics and YouTube Analytics and www.bit.ly.

- **The Call to Action:** Adams quotes Tony Robbins, **"If there's no action, you haven't truly decided."** Your virus needs a Call for Action; else what's the commercial point? Why should your virus's host do anything? **Motivation.** "What's in it for me?" [WIIFM] Try "free," a known motivator. "What's in it for free?" [WIIFF] Free TV is paid for by advertisers. Ditto Facebook and Twitter. The rub is, "Without being remarkable you cannot go viral...."

- **How to Build Your Virus:** Start with passion, though not for your own profit. Add uniqueness. Plus value. Then simplicity. Easy? If it were, more would succeed in creating them. **Target** your virus's **hosts-to-be.** Think about their demographics and lifestyles. **Fill a void.** Provide a solution, entertain, or advise. **Keep it simple,** easy to use, easy to digest. **Add unique value. Create a story,** like Susan Boyle's rags-to-riches saga. Add a **Call to Action,** "above the fold," prominently. **Develop a relationship...** woo your audience, warm them up. Recall: **know, like, trust.**

- **How to Spread Your Virus:** "Marketing...is a conversation," sharing stories. You must **interact and engage** with the crowd. Don't just "say something and walk away."

Viral nearly unanimously got very favorable reviews at amazon. com, where it is available for about $3 as an ebook and $6 as a paperback, 118 pages long.

CHAPTER 5

PAYOFF

*A mind that has been stretched
will never return to its original dimension.*
Albert Einstein

Your payoff from writing your book will depend on your goals,
your actions, your environment, and luck. Self-satisfaction
comes first, from a sense of accomplishment, a sense of personal growth. Seeing that others learn from what you have
written brings additional pleasure. Changing minds, thanking
those who have helped you, criticizing those who have fallen
short...all add to your sense of well-being. Furthermore, your
book may actually make you a net profit, directly or indirectly.

WAYS TO MAKE MONEY FROM WRITING A BOOK (CANFIELD, BOLT, HARRISON)

The *Chicken Soup...* series of books primarily co-authored by
Jack Canfield and Mark Victor Hansen are a major source of
Canfield's more than 500 million books sold. Even if his royalties were only a dollar per book, we would not be talking
chicken feed, but real money, money most authors never come
close to earning.

What follows is derived from the March 8, 2012, telephone seminar by Canfield, "How to Get Where You Want As an Author/Speaker," part of a series sponsored by Steve Harrison's Bradley Communications group, whose teaching programs are available through yourquantumleap.com. These teaching programs Canfield credits for getting him well started in his writing/marketing career.

Later, I Googled "chicken soup for the soul," an early bestseller, and got 17 million hits. Here's a surprise: Canfield and Hansen were rejected by 144 publishers before they got one who agreed to publish their book, making that obscure publishing house's owner a multi-millionaire.

Rejected by one hundred and forty-four publishers and yet they persevered! It still took eighteen months for their book to make the bestseller lists. During that time, Canfield and Hansen studied such successful authors as Ken Blanchard, Scott Peck, John Gray *et al.* They looked for patterns in successful promotions. Eventually, they reached #1 on the *NY Times* bestseller list and sold over 10 million copies of the English-language version alone.

Canfield had been a school teacher, dedicated to motivating his students, often by raising their self-esteem. His mission became to inspire and empower people to live to their highest visions with love and joy. He has done well by trying to do good.

He said that some secrets of his success include:

1. **Big goals are needed.**
2. **Envision future achievements.**

3. Make your own luck; attract it.
4. Meditate.
5. Don't be reluctant to sell what you have created.
6. Provide solutions for people.
7. Make your goals specific and challenging.

Canfield quoted Gen. Wesley Clark, **"It takes no more time to dream a big dream than to dream a small one."**

Canfield was also influenced by Chicago billionaire business-man W. Clement Stone:

1. **Think big.**
2. **Do it now.**
3. **Visualize success and affirm that you will achieve it.**
4. **See #2.**

To succeed, one must give. Canfield and crew specify a specific charity to receive some of the proceeds of each book. You have to give to get. What goes around, comes around, and often these charities have helped publicize the books to their members. Non-members like the idea that some of the book price goes to a good cause. One hand, it seems, washes the other. Often, Canfield and Hansen have donated articles they have written or chapters from their books, and have given away untold numbers of their books to those who will help spread the good words.

Authors, he emphasized, must get out of their offices and talk with people if they hope to increase their book sales. Join organizations. Network. Read *Speak and Grow Rich* by Dottie and Lillie Walters (1997). Talk beats print for selling.

Canfield greatly benefited from Bradley Communications boss Steve Harrison's *Radio-TV Interview Report,* which helped him to do over 600 interviews his first year. After that, he "cut back" to about 300 per year, some interviews lasting as long as one hour. These longer ones proved the most productive.

According to Canfield: Can't get bookstores to let you have a book signing? Not to worry. **Only 1 out of 7 Americans go to a bookstore in a year.** Look for other places to put your books, depending on topic. Any place where people wait is a candidate, and you split the profit with the proprietor or even let him have it all, as word-of-mouth advertising is precious.

Chandler Bolt subtitled his excellent Amazon Kindle ebook, *Book Launch,* **"How to write, market, and self-publish your first bestseller in 3 months or less AND use it to start and grow a six-figure income."**

Bolt notes: an Amazon ebook becomes a one-click "impulse buy that's being promoted and marketed by the biggest brands in the world," with unlimited, free distribution and unlimited shelf space.

Here are Bolt's seven ways:

- **Passive income from book sales.** Your ebook can be read almost anywhere, anytime. Amazon Kindle will give you 70% of the purchase price between $2.99 and $9.99 and 35% of the price below $2.99 or above $9.99.
- **Leads for your business.** Your book advertises your business.
- **More coaching clients and speaking gigs.** "…no bet-

ter way to increase your fee, book more speaking gigs, and land more coaching clients than through a book." It makes you an authority.

- **Free exposure and PR for your business.** Publications, radio, TV...the book gives you an entrée, a reason to be interviewed. Each appearance improves the likelihood of another, somewhere.
- **Build/grow your business.** Bolt built a business he did not originally have, based on his first book. Your book is a "salesman in print that's constantly building relationships with buyers...." **Grow your network.** "These days, a book is like a glorified business card....when was the last time you threw away a book?" Get past their gate-keepers, "...mail a copy of your book to their door...."
- **Grow your local business.** Your book gives you added credibility, home and away.

Heed another prosperous author: John Gray, who wrote the multi-million-book bestseller _Men Are from Mars, Women Are from Venus,_ was interviewed by Steve Harrison of Bradley Communications, who present a year-long training program for 100 authors who want to become millionaires, too. [See their site, yourquantumleap.com.]

Harrison sends me multitudinous emails with useful information as part of the campaign to get each year's one hundred students registered for the program. No doubt the program is valuable, to the attendees and to the Bradley Communications company.

Authors, like myself, dream of being as successful as John

Gray. Whether we can replicate the process that got him there is not so clear. Before becoming a famous writer, for example, John Gray spent nine years as a monk. I'll skip doing that. He has written 16 books, of which only one has had exceptional success. *Men Are from Mars…* was written at a time when people thought, at least you were supposed to think, that men and women are nearly identical. Doll houses for little boys and guns for little girls were sometimes recommended. Gray's message was simple: men and women are very different, more different than people from different countries, almost as though they come from different planets.

To be a successful author, Gray maintains, you need to give a new perspective, with passion. To be a successful author, you must not only write a worthwhile book, you must promote yourself and the book, and market it successfully.

In fact, a successful book is not likely to be enough to give you the luxurious lifestyle you might envision for yourself. Instead, you need something to follow up, perhaps more books, but more likely special programs, such as training programs for people in general or perhaps for authors specifically.

Ideally, you would have done substantial groundwork, such as presenting workshops, before writing and publishing your book. John Gray, having left the monastery, worked as a computer programmer, then as a coach, giving workshops on interpersonal relationships.

The original source material for *Men Are from Mars…* was titled *Men, Women and Relationships*. Gray says that the original's text was much too long, even though it did sell 50,000 copies in its first year. A book agent was willing to represent Gray, and in fact found him due to a seminar that Gray had given.

Gray came to realize that his book needed to be substantially shorter, and he took something like the best dozen of roughly a hundred concepts, and wrote them up in a friendly fashion, easy to read. Men might be described as "martial," a word derived from "Mars," and they see themselves as problem-solvers. Women could be described as from Venus, seeking partners, not problem-solvers.

Even though, as events proved, the ideas in the book were right for the time, it took another year after it was published before it made the *New York Times* bestseller list.

Once *Men Are from Mars...* left the bestseller list, some seven years later, Gray found himself somewhat depressed. He soon learned, however, that one can make more money from activities related to the book, such as seminars and training, than one may make from the book itself.

Gray advises new authors that radio and TV, especially radio, can be successful venues for book promotion, as long as you have something fresh, with "a hook," like his Mars-Venus analogy. Jack Canfield made similar points.

I appreciate the free training materials that I've gotten from Steve Harrison's company, Bradley Communications, and other providers of writer training programs. Although I was very pleased with my own first book, *Ting and I: A Memoir of Love, Courage, and Devotion*, it has not flown off the shelves. I have done most of the things that have been recommended for promoting the book, and I have gotten some local publicity in the form of newspaper articles and magazine articles, yet sales have been slow.

A year from now, Harrison's program will have nearly another 100 graduates. Will there be room on the bestseller list for all of them? Successful authors can tell us what they did, and they can sincerely believe that what they did caused their success. What we don't know is how many other authors did much the same things and were never heard of.

Still, if one doesn't try, one will never succeed. A few players shorter than six-feet tall have played in the National Basketball Association. How did they make it? Later, did they end up giving seminars on that, too? How many tried and failed and were never heard from?

I heard another terrific telephone seminar by Steve Harrison, the title of which was, **"Seven Things That Rich Authors Do Differently from Poor Authors."** Actually, Harrison added an eighth key to authorial financial success. To give Steve and his brother Bill Harrison their due, let me recommend that you go to their website: *yourquantumleap.com* and sign up for their future offerings.

The kind of book under discussion here is a nonfiction book that logically lends itself to some formulation as a "How To..." offering.

Steve Harrison asks what business we as authors think we're in. The answer is that we are primarily going to have to be in marketing and promotion and public relations if we are to disseminate our tools, our information, our good advice to those who would profit from the same.

Here are eight keys, paraphrasing Steve Harrison's talk:

1. **A good book does not in general sell itself. You need a marketing plan.**
2. **An author should promote not only his book but other offerings.** Examples were given of the expensive [$195] game marketed by the author of *Rich Dad, Poor Dad*; food supplements marketed by the author of *Body for Life*; and the various offerings of the late Stephen Covey whose *The 7 Habits of Highly Effective People* yearly ranks high on the bestseller lists and who got $65,000 per speech.
3. **More valuable than the copyright on your book is the list of customers who bought your book.** From that list you can make offers which eventually will produce income. You have to be setting up to be able to offer something to those whose names and addresses you capture this way.
4. **As part of your book, perhaps as an appendix, you should be offering services and / or products, or at least soliciting e-mail addresses** so that you can contact them later with such offerings.
5. **Where possible, try to sell the books in volume to organizations** rather than one-by-one to individuals. A good example is the success that this technique has brought the author of *The Purpose-Driven Life*, Rick Warren.
6. **The publicity that you can generate from a news event or an interview is not enough.** You need to find other methods of exposure, such as writing articles, having a website, having a blog, entering into a joint venture,

presenting tele-seminars such as the one I just listened to along with 1200 other attendees, regular seminars, a radio or television show, a newsletter.

7. **In general, the real money is not to be made from book sale profits but rather from follow-up activities such as training workshops.** An example was given of a woman who puts on 10 weekend workshops a year, getting 15 attendees at $1200 per person.

8. **Finally, don't operate alone.** Develop a support team. Hire others, work with interns, find designers, use temporary help, whatever is necessary to get the job done.

He suggested that as a memory aid you think of the word "FAME:"

- **Focus your plan** for the next 90 days.
- **A lot more exposure** needs to be obtained.
- **Models proven to work** must be your guide.
- **Execute.**

The tele-seminar was informative and interesting. I presume that the Harrison's get their benefit by the mailing list that they develop through those who register at their site, yourquantumleap. com. Some who register will likely become paying students of theirs.

HOW TO MAKE A LIVING WITH YOUR WRITING: BOOKS, BLOGGING, AND MORE (PENN, 2015)

A decade or so ago, Joanna Penn gave up a lucrative, cubicle-encased career as a management consultant, a surprising venue for a woman with a theology degree, and became an independent author, now making annually in the "six-figure" region, half of it from her indie-published books and the other half from offshoots thereof. The Contents list from her "How-To" book follow:

- **Yes, it is possible!**
- **Overview: How I make a living with my writing.**
- **First principles**
- **Tips on writing and productivity**
- **Tips on mindset**

PART 1: How to Make Money from Books

- It's not just one book!
- Your publishing options
- Traditional publishing
- Changes in the publishing industry
- Your publishing options: becoming an indie author
- How to self-publish an ebook
- How to self-publish an audiobook
- How to actually make money with books

PART 2. How to make Money Online in Other Ways

- A business powered by content marketing
- Product sales
- Affiliate income
- Consulting or coaching
- Professional speaking
- Advertising and sponsorship
- Tips for content marketing
- The transition and your next steps:

We're focused here primarily on books, though making money in related areas is not to be sneered at. You should get her book if you don't want to be the traditional starving (though often happily drunk) writer.

First principles: "Think of yourself as an entrepreneur" and create value for others. **"Focus on creating scalable income."** Rather than earning an hourly wage, be susceptible to big success or at least money from a variety of ways of packaging what your write (different media, languages} and thus **"develop multiple streams of income." "Think global, digital, and mobile."** Technology and tastes change. **"Decide on your definition of success."** Must you really be published by Harper and be in the running for big-name prizes?

Online resources she cites: Tim Ferriss podcast, Kristine Kathryn Busch Business blog, Sell More Books Show podcast, Self-publishing Advice blog from the Alliance of Independent Authors, and a half-dozen more.

Penn (2015) shows why using a traditional publisher has not attracted her. There is too much delay, too little author control, too many opportunities for the contract to be worded to the author's disadvantage, taking away rights to potential revenue streams. As the workers at a Harvard University protest once noted, "You can't eat prestige." Much the same objection can be raised concerning traditional publishing. You do get editorial help and direction, and some advance money, and a modest amount of marketing. "Once you sign a contract for your book, it essentially belongs to the publisher...." Enough said?

Ebook purchases at, for example, Amazon, have outnumbered print books since 2012. Many people find it easier to carry their ebook reader than lug or store printed books. Penn (2015) covers pros and cons of the publishing options, and we have outlined them here elsewhere.

Elements for publishing success, per Penn (2015): a great book, an enticing title, a brilliant cover, a compelling sales description, and an attractive ebook format. As she notes, many authors (present company included) do not want to mess with the details of formatting the ebooks for distribution. See her book for more about all this.

Penn (2015) gives details for self-publishing a print book and an audiobook, but we leave those tidbits for authors interested in getting down and dirty with technology, with her help.

A more interesting section to me is "How to actually make money with books," and I quote:

- *Write more books*
- *Write books that people want to buy: by genre or category*
- *Write books that people want to buy: by search terms*
- *Write a series and get people hooked*
- *Think global, digital, mobile and long-term*

- *Write in multiple genres and multiple lengths*
- *Consider the up-sell [Anyone want a writing coach?]*
- *Grow your own email list [A legal "crop" in 50 states.]*

But what if your book, isn't selling? Rayne Hall (2015) has some answers next.

20 SIMPLE FIXES IF YOUR BOOK ISN'T SELLING (HALL, 2015):

Although I have covered some of these in earlier parts of this book, I list here Hall's 20 fixes for why one's book does not sell. She devotes a chapter to each:

- the book cover
- the blurb
- sample pages
- link detours
- know your reader
- targeting versus scattershot
- permission versus intrusion
- buried in cemeteries
- social media
- websites, blogs and other time sinks
- stop obsessing over what doesn't matter
- how to get real book reviews
- end-matter excerpts
- shared marketing
- once-effective methods no longer work
- distribution channels
- focused efforts to achieve more
- change the title

- the opening scene
- freshen up your writing voice

Let's look at some of these we have yet to discuss:

- **Sample Pages:** Some book promotion sites allow you to select a percentage of your book to display, the first 10%, 20%, etc. Make sure your book's "good stuff" fits there. Be generous.
- **Link Detours:** Every time you ask readers to click on a link to go somewhere else, a large fraction refuse to do so. You've lost them. Make your links usually go to where the book is sold.
- **Know Your Reader:** Define your prime demographics. Where do they hang out?
- **Targeting vs. Scattershot:** Promote your book to your target audience, or you are wasting time, money, and effort. Go where your readers will be.
- **Permission vs. Intrusion:** Hall, "Most advertising is unwelcome. It intrudes...." Some advertising is welcome, though, as people have agreed to receive it, like mail-order catalogs. Intrusion advertising repels, and permission advertising attracts. Broadcasted advertising can easily devolve into spam, making the advertiser unpopular, even a pariah.
- **Buried in Cemeteries:** Don't advertise where there are lots of other similar advertisers, or you will not stand out. Don't pay to be on a site which just promotes books, rather than supplies material that will attract readers.
- **Social Media:** Hall notes, "Every social media message is a mini-sample of your writing." Remember that. Create interesting posts, but not merely about your book, al-

though writing about related content makes sense. Avoid automated Tweet schemes.

- **Websites, Blogs and Other Time-Sinks**. Hall writes, "You need an Internet presence, a way for publishers, journalists and fans to contact you. But you may not need as much as you think….and where do you take the time from? It's the time you would otherwise spend writing books." Consider closing an ineffectual blog and guest-blogging instead. Keep your website up to date...or close it down. Online groups are often time-wasters.

- **Stop Obsessing Over What Doesn't Matter**. Good advice in general. Search Engine Optimization (SEO) is irrelevant for writers. Forego social media ranking games. Do try to get ranked high in some Amazon sub-genre categories, however, Hall maintains, as readers will often be influenced by that. Be a big fish in a small pond to get noticed. You'll have to contact Amazon to get your categories changed. Use all the keywords you can.

- **How to Get Real Book Reviews**: Readers are influenced by the number and enthusiasm of book reviews a book receives. Hall's suggestions: Ask your beta readers for reviews; at the end of your book, ask your reader for reviews; when fans contact you, ask them for reviews. Offer free ebooks, but nothing else, for reviews. Don't respond to reviews, Hall writes, whether positive or negative. Don't buy reviews ever. Don't swap reviews with other authors. Don't have friends sabotage competitors.

- **End-Matter Excerpts:** If a reader has finished and liked a book, he is likely to buy a similar one he is exposed to with an excerpt at the end of the book he just read. Add an excerpt from your next book or arrange to swap excerpts with an author in the same genre.

- **Shared Marketing:** Hall writes: *When you join forces with another indie author, you can halve your marketing workload and double your results—but only if you choose the right partner.* I find that on Twitter, much the same effect is obtained by posting to hashtags like #promocave and #amwriting.

- **Once-Effective Methods No Longer Work:** The original becomes conventional. The rare becomes common. Free books glut the market. Circumstances change. Hall: "By the time you copy someone else's success technique, it's already useless." Let's hope her advice lasts longer than that. She recommends you try what has worked, but stop if it no longer works or does not work for you.

- **Distribution Channels:** Conventional publishing relied on the path publishers-distributors-bookshops-reader. Now indie authors sell online, choosing their own channels, preferably Amazon, Barnes & Noble, Apple, *etc.* **"Most new authors sell far more ebooks than paperbacks, so make sure your book is available in electronic format."(Hall, 2015)**

- **Focused Efforts Achieve More**: Success breeds success. Investing in reaching the ranking of #3 from #30 pays better than moving from #3000 to #2000, Hall maintains, so place your money and efforts on your near-winner rather than your also-rans. Concentrated promotion beats long-term.

- **Change the Title**: See earlier discussion on titles. Note this change in your book descriptions.

- **The Opening Scene**: Hall (2015): "Many new authors' novels begin with the same few openings." Avoid.

- **Freshen Up Your Writing Voice:** Use less common words, but not arcane ones.

GETTING PUBLISHED AND SELLING BOOKS ON AMAZON (COHEN, 2015)

In May 2015, Ty Cohen, highly successful author of books sold as paperbacks primarily on amazon.com and as ebooks sold through its Kindle Direct Publishing Program (KDP), presented a generously detailed webinar on writing and publishing his way, followed with a short pitch for his program that you can see at KindleCashFlow.com.

He has been dubbed "King of Amazon Kindle Publishing" and has sold hundreds of thousands of copies of his works.

I summarize his talk:

What's Your Problem?

New authors typically have one of the following three problems:

1. **Being a procrastinating perfectionist. The writer finds his work is never perfect, so he never publishes it.**
2. **Not knowing what the audience wants.**
3. **Needing a way to get in front of the right audience.**

These new authors have other problems, as well, with decisions that need to be made about: attracting readers, setting prices, choosing covers, selecting genres, and getting started rapidly.

Prospects for Publishing

Publishing is undergoing a radical transformation from the publishing of physical books to the publishing of digital books:

1. The book *50 Shades of Grey* got its initial success on Amazon's Kindle.
2. Amanda Hocking made $3 million in her first 18 months; she was self-published.
3. Stephen Leather sells 2000 ebooks per day containing his novellas.
4. Novelist John Locke sold $1 million in ebooks in his first year, under nine different titles.

Clearly there is money, distribution, even fame to be obtained through the use of self-publishing in digital media.

Keys to the Kingdom and Its Treasury

Ty Cohen's keys to success on Amazon:

1. **Discover what readers want.**
2. **Determined which price points are optimal.**
3. **Build a huge, loyal fan base.**
4. **Generate large sales so readers and publishers seek you out.**

Amazon's royalties dwarf those of traditional publishing houses. Often Amazon gives authors 70% of the price of their ebook. Conventional publishers typically give 5 to 10% royalty for a printed book.

Not only are there 7 billion devices worldwide that can receive ebook content, but Amazon itself has 700 million credit card numbers already on file, simplifying the purchasing process for its customers.

Use Amazon for Research

Authors can use Amazon's sales information and review information to determine what the public is interested in having them write about.

Go to amazon.com and type in the genre you want to investigate. Sort by the number of reviews that the books have received or more specifically five-star and four-star reviews. Amazon makes it easy to sort by other characteristics as well.

Look at the most popular books and determine their strengths and weaknesses by reading the very favorable and the very unfavorable reviews. This will help you understand what the readers want and don't want.

In general, the book's title is the first thing that captures a potential reader's attention. Next is the cover. Finally, those still interested will read the description of the book.

Give Them What They Want

You are trying to seduce your reader into going past page 20. The title beckons. The first few pages continue to entice. You must continue to battle for attention.

Price Wisely

Although a high price will give you more money per book, it can easily become too high and cut your total revenue. **Amazon gives 70% for ebooks priced at $2.99 and above, and this $2.99 price Cohen has found to be optimal. Books over $10 sell at 1/6th the** rate of those at $2.99. Not only does this $2.99 price get your more money up front, it gets more readers to swell your fan base, valuable for sales of follow-on publications and other uses.

In pricing the paperback edition of my *WYBWM*, I chose to make it roughly $1.50 more than the minimum allowed by its publisher. Gaining wider distribution trumped profit-making. If I make it a Kindle book, I will probably charge $2.99, as lower prices produce much less income, and very inexpensive books are often not given much respect. Besides, 70% of $2.99 nets the author $2.09, and 35% of $0.99 nets $0.35, one-sixth.

Get Many Honest Positive Reviews

The number of reviews the book has and how enthusiastic they are keys to successful sales. Even if you are giving the book away, people will be reluctant to spend the time to read them without some reasonable assurance that they are likely to find that effort worthwhile. Favorable reviews give that reassurance.

How to obtain such reviews?

1. **Write a good book.**
2. **Contact people who have already written reviews on Amazon.** [Some top reviewers have profiles with contact information, as may some who have reviewed books similar to yours.]
3. **Having contacted them, ask if they would like a copy, and gently request that they review it.** Those who do agree to accept a copy of the book will usually end up giving favorable reviews, partly because they are predisposed to liking such books and partly due to feeling that a gift should be reciprocated.

Use Translations to Speak to Reader in Own Language

Second to English is Spanish for world-wide use, and English books can be translated to Spanish readily using http://translate.google.com or hiring a translator from eLance.com or UpWork.com.

Create Your Own Amazon KDP Account

Amazon provides some free instructions or one can pay for more detailed help from Ty Cohen's site at http://KindleCashFlow.com/go.

9 MISTAKES MOST AUTHORS MAKE (HARRISON, 2015)

On January 16, 2015, I listened to a fine webinar by marketing and publicity expert Steve Harrison (@PublicityGuy on Twitter, head of Bradley Communications Corp.) on nine common errors, to which he added a tenth. He emphasized that **your book represents you, so make it as good as you can.**

The errors:

1. **WRONG STRUCTURE:** Don't deviate from the tried and true, such classics as Covey's itemized *7 Habits of Highly Effective People,* Blanchard's parables in the *One-Minute Manager,* or the classic *How To....* Imitate what has succeeded in the past.
2. **WRONG PUBLISHING OPTION:** Your choices include self-publishing, co-publishing with a subsidy press, getting an agent and a conventional publisher. Then, too, there are print and digital. Each has its plusses and minuses.

3. **WRONG TITLE:** Keep it short. Make it intriguing. Make a promise. Bust a myth. Quantify, such as Tim Ferriss did in *The 4-Hour Work Week.* Get advice from others; even run a focus group.

4. **NOT MEDIA-GENIC:** Need a hook to get attention: Fame. Celebrity. Current event. How to. Myth busting. Controversy.

5. **WAIT UNTIL PUBLISHED TO START CASHING-IN**: No, start as soon as you have a good title and some work done on the book. Pre-sell, if you can. Lecture. Do interviews.

6. **TRYING TO SAY EVERYTHING IN ONE BOOK**: Pick your best, save the rest. A few key ideas you can explain clearly, forcefully.

7. **NOT IDENTIFYING A "CHOIR" TO PREACH TO THAT WILL SING YOUR PRAISES**: Need a tribe to help promote you. Rick Warren's *Purpose-Driven Life* advanced by congregations he contacted. Robert Kiyosaki (2000) pushed *Rich Dad, Poor Dad* with help from multi-level marketing contacts.

8. **NOT DESIGNING YOUR BOOK TO FACILITATE FOLLOW-UPS:** Make it easy to know how to reach you. Solicit email addresses from fans. Much money from books comes from follow-up activities, like speeches.

9. **NOT HAVING A TEAM:** Rome wasn't built in a day, nor single-handedly. Others help with ideas and actions, serve as "multipliers."

10. **PERFECTIONISM:** Promising nine items, Harrison delivered one more: the French say, "the best is the enemy of the good." Nothing man-made is perfect, and if you wait to reach perfection, you will not publish.

SELL MORE BOOKS (ALLEN, 2015)

Mark Allen subtitled this little ebook *Self-Publisher's Guide to Getting a Top Selling Book,* and charges only $0.99 at amazon. com, for its 40 pages of material.

Top Selling Book is all about how to market a self-published book....based on the following basic ideas:

- Book Expansion
- Social Media
- YouTube
- Blogging
- Other Media (podcasts, radio TV)

Each idea is meant to market and expand awareness of your book.

Each element helps support the other.

Book Expansion

His first idea: work hard to get your book on the first page of searches by giving it away or selling it cheaply at the start.

This will help with his second recommendation: get reviews. The more readers, the more reviews. Top reviewers at amazon display their email addresses, and you are urged to contact them. Put the link to Amazon's review page for the book at the end of your book, where those who read it to the end will find it conveniently.

"Your book should be offered to all major ebook vendors. At

the end of this book, I have a large list with links to eBook sites."

Consider turning your ebook into a physical book, using for example, Create Space. You can buy them cut-rate and sell them in person.

Offer your book as an app.

Do an audio book, perhaps getting a voice-over from someone on fiverr.com.

Social Media

"…it can generate as much as 60% of your monthly sales."

He lists the top ten sites and the number of their unique monthly visitors.

"Social media is global word of mouth. Books get sold on word of mouth." "Don't get discouraged. Growing an audience is slow." "Don't spam shameless plugs for your book."

YouTube

"YouTube marketing is effective for nonfiction and fiction books alike. Especially 'how to' type YouTube videos." The videos have a long shelf life. Consider using a pro from fiverr, although audiences may prefer the author.

Blogs

"For fiction and nonfiction alike, an author blog is a must

have." The free blogs are probably adequate. You want to catch the attention of people. "You attract people with your information and direct them in one way of another to your book and branding." You have to use other social media to call attention to your blog. Search for related blogs and contribute there.

Giving

"The more you give to people, the more sales you will get."

Stay Global

Time spent marketing broadly is a better investment than marketing locally. Think: Pareto's 80/20 rule, 80% of the value in 20% of the items/activities.

List of eBook Sites

About 80 are listed, and their links are active, using the Kindle.

SELLING YOUR FIRST 1000 COPIES (GRAHL, 2013)

Your First 1000 Copies: The Step-by-Step Guide to Marketing Your Book is Tim Grahl's contribution to the art or science of marketing your book. His method relies on a strong email list, applying a system of:

Permission: "Without permission, your communication efforts risk being ignored, deleted or otherwise tuned out." Grahl's key: a mailing list of willing recipients. "**Earning such permission is the art of motivating website visitors to grant permission to stay connected.**" In other words, letting you add to the clutter of their email. "Having a direct connection to an individual's inbox gives authors a way to communicate to their readers where they regularly spend their time."

You get their permission by attracting them to a website with an offer, exchanging the offer for something you value, their email address. **People pay more attention to most items in their email inbox, nearly 100%, than they do to items on Twitter or Facebook, more like 1%.** You want them to get to know you and vice-versa. **"…your #1 goal as an author should be to grow your email list as much as possible."** Look into MailChimp, Aweber, and Constant Contact.

"…two overarching rules: (1) make a specific, compelling offer and (2) expose them to the offer multiple times."

Content: Use their permission; deliver to them valuable content regularly, and share it freely and publicly, giving it a chance to go viral. Share more than you feel comfortable sharing. Grahl (2013) gives many examples of success by sharing: as your following grows faster, your connections increase and improve, and your reputation soars. Consider bonus offerings besides the book. "Fans want more."

Outreach: Expanding and deepening your connections, outreach, starts with empathy, identifying with the feelings and thoughts of another. Help others. Zig Zigler is quoted, "You can get everything you want in life if you just help enough other people to get what they want in life." Grahl claims the investment is worth it: "Long-term career plans require long-term thinking." Over time, you will have connections to both fans and influencers, the latter being more lucrative. **Fans** you give one-to-many communication. **Influencers** you give one-to-one interaction.

For recruiting readers, Grahl recommends:

1. **Profile your readers.**
2. **Identify where they spend their time.**
3. **Create an introduction approach to their platform**(s).

Selling: This is the goal of the system. Boost yourself. Ask others to buy, having stimulated their appetites. "Leave them wanting more." Tell stories that help you connect emotionally with your readers. "Enthusiasm sells. Let it out." Make it easy to buy and ask them to.

Building the system: Mass marketing especially depends on building a system to manage the multitudinous contacts. Do it.

Unfortunately, this is not the kind of work I like to do; My email list is paltry and filled with friends rather than potential customers. Your talents, taste, and experience may be quite different.

Another kind of work I do not do is described next.

GHOSTWRITING GHASTLINESS?

I almost got paid to write some books rather than to coach or edit. For nearly a day this prospect had me feeling high.

A representative from "Fake Publishing" (not its actual name) contacted me on Twitter, where I am active in writing about politics, science, and writing. He indicated he had liked what he had read of mine, went to my site, writeyourbookwithme. com, and liked that, too. He asked whether I would be interested in getting paid to write books for his company.

I responded that, depending on the topic, this would suit me just fine, and I offered to do so for a few cents per word. He continued to be interested, and we scheduled a phone conversation for the following morning. Excited, I went through my 300-odd blog entries and my monthly articles for asiancemagazine.com and my memoir, *Ting and I,* and came up with dozens of possible topics I could write up for them. I assumed we would be discussing his needs and my suggestions and come to a "meeting of the minds" on a topic. Money was not my paramount consideration, although it is the sincerest form of flattery.

When we spoke the next day, it became clear that what he wanted was ghostwriting. He said he was impressed with my credentials and my writing and that Fake Publishing has orders for books that professionals, like doctors, pay to have others write for them. **The real author is to be a "ghost," not to be credited in any way, but rather the "professional" is to be the person associated with the book.**

I said I would not do this for two reasons: First, some credit (even in the acknowledgments) is part of the reward for writing the book. Second, and more important to me, participating in what I see as fraud is distasteful. Claiming credit for a book one did not write is a form a plagiarism, big time, despite its being quite common—for politician's books, for example.

Years ago I helped a very successful writer who had gotten wealthy, partly through ghostwriting books. He paid me for the bulk of my contributions, which he used for part of the book he was writing for a doctor, but he stiffed me for the last 20% of what I wrote. I was helping him ghostwrite a book. Perhaps I was aiding and abetting fraud. I should not have been surprised that, to a degree, he cheated me, too. **The adage goes, "You can't cheat an honest man." I might add, you are likely to be cheated when dealing with a dishonest person.**

If you are dealing with a professional who claims to have written a book, beware. Check his publishing company out, if you can. I'd give you this advice: **don't trust a plagiarist or his enablers.**

GHOSTWRITING DEFENDED (CARTER, 2015)

Mine may be a minority view, especially among writers, so I asked my British writer friend, Ginny Carter, if I could quote her recent letter sent to those on her mailing list, concerning how and why she ghostwrites. It follows:

Working with a book ghostwriter—the how and why

I'm sure you've heard about ghostwriters. They're those slightly mysterious creatures who pen other peoples' books for them, writing their content in their voice. They don't have their name on the book (that accolade belongs to the author), but they do get to talk to a lot of interesting people. Maybe you've thought of hiring one yourself, or possibly you feel a bit suspicious about the whole thing and wonder why someone wouldn't write their own book.

I'll admit, when I first started my ghostwriting and book coaching business, I wondered too. Would people would be ok with the idea of asking a professional to write in their voice? It turns out, they would!

That's because there are some serious advantages to this particular way of creating your book.

As an aside, many of our most well-known and most loved business books contain acknowledgements for ghostwriter assistance. Examples are: Stephen Covey in The 7 Habits of Highly Effective People, Donald Trump in The Art of The Deal, and Richard Branson in Losing My Virginity.

Why use a ghostwriter to write your business book?

For a start, it saves the author time. Time they can spend more

productively on the business tasks only they can do. They don't have to get up at 5am every morning to fit in a thousand words before breakfast—they can simply hand the heavy lifting to someone else to do it for them. This means they can focus on preparing the marketing for their book launch, and planning how they're going to make the most of their book to build their expert reputation once it's published.

In other words, hiring a ghostwriter might be the difference between a book being written, and it staying in the author's head (where it's not a lot of use to anyone).

Secondly, for many business people writing isn't their main strength—and why should it be? Worrying whether your sentences are flowing and your ideas are coming across clearly and persuasively can feel like a chore. I'm a big believer in outsourcing whatever you can. For instance, I'm terrible with numbers so I've always had an accountant; she saves me hours of time and makes sure my figures add up correctly, so I can sleep at night knowing they're being taken care of.

Most folks are comfortable with the above, but sometimes it leads to the next question …

Isn't using a ghostwriter a bit like cheating?

Here's the thing. As a ghostwriter, I can (and will) only write my author's own thoughts, ideas and opinions. I'll also write them in the way they'd most like them expressed. Sure, I'll add my own creativity and writing skills into the mix, making sure their train of thought is expressed in the best possible way. And I'll speak up when I see things going off track. But the book comes from the author, not me.

In fact, the very process of working with a business book ghostwriter means my clients have to get crystal clear on their core message and why it matters (something I help them with as we plan the book).

Are there any disadvantages to using a ghostwriter?

For some business owners, writing their book themselves is really important to them; they want the personal satisfaction that comes from being both author and writer. The DIY approach can be a great learning experience and very rewarding, and also entails a lower financial investment.

So how does using a business book ghostwriter work?

I can't speak for all of us ghostwriters, but this is my process:

1) *I sit down and work out the book's strategy with my client: what the book's big idea is, who it's for, how these two factors fit together, whether there's a market for the book, and most importantly how it's going to help their business.*

2) *We work out an outline, using their content as a starting point.*

3) *I interview them via Skype. In these interviews, I draw out the story from my client that's bigger and better than the one they would have found within them. Having a warm and trusting relationship is key for this, and it can be an enjoyable part of the process for the author.*

4) *The calls are recorded and transcribed. These transcriptions, together with any written or audio material my client already has, form the raw material for the book. The recordings and transcriptions also help me to capture the tone and language used, so I can write in their voice.*

5) *I write each chapter, sending them for feedback as we go along.*

6) *We both review, creating around 3 drafts in total.*

7) *The manuscript is proof read and handed to my client. If he/she wants, I help them publish and market it as well.*

And that's it, really. It seems pretty simple now, doesn't it? Have you ever thought of working with a ghostwriter to create your book? How would you feel about it?

Ginny Carter
"The Author Maker"
ginny@marketingtwentyone.co.uk

Having read Ginny's explanation of what she does, I must admit that, as she has written to me, I am "closer to being a ghostwriter than [I] think." Since the famous authors she cited seem to have mentioned their writers in their acknowledgments, my biggest objection was met: they publicly did give some credit. Getting one's name on the cover and title page is more valuable still, but now we are talking about degrees of recognition. Thank you, Ginny.

CHAPTER 6

REFLECTIONS

Life can only be lived forwards,
but it can only be understood backwards.
Soren Kierkegaard

HOW TO BE OUTSTANDING (SHUFELDT, 2013)

In his recently published *The Ingredients of Outliers,* physician-lawyer-businessman **John Shufeldt, MD, JD, MBA, has written a succinct recipe book for personal achievement, for becoming outstanding,** an "outlier," in your field. In statistics, an "outlier" is a rare case, and in life, outstanding excellence is rare and treasured.

Dr. Shufeldt's section headings and my comments follow:

HUMILITY: The Root of Success

Dr. Shufeldt gives examples from his life of instances where ego has gotten in the way of success. Teachers will tell you that you cannot learn what you think you already know. The *Bible* admonishes, **"Pride goeth before a fall." "Egotism is the glue with which you get stuck on yourself,"** according to writer Dan

Post. Inspirational author Vernon Howard advised, "Extinguish the ego." Poet Rudyard Kipling urged us to view seeming success and seeming failure as two "impostors," and not be swayed by them. An unrealistic view of ourselves is unattractive and can lead to serious miscalculations.

FAIL FAST: The Gift of Failure

"All successful people were failures along their journey—the only difference is that they learned and persevered," writes Dr. Shufeldt. Recall that Abraham Lincoln lost several elections before becoming President of the United States. If you are always succeeding, you are probably not challenging yourself enough, not reaching for sufficiently high goals. We can learn from our failures but not from inaction. **Marian Wright Edelman is cited as noting, "Failure is just another way to learn how to do something right."** The more you try, even if failing, the more you learn, and quicker is better.

PERSISTENCE: Press On!

Dr. Shufeldt begins this section by **recalling the courageous persistence of George Washington and the Continental Army in its War for Independence from Britain,** during most of which conditions were brutal and defeat seemed likely. Billionaire industrialist H. Ross Perot is quoted as lamenting, "Most people give up just when they are about to achieve success. They quit on the one-yard line...just a foot from a winning touchdown." I love the quote from **American essayist Christopher Morley, "Big shots are only little shots who keep on shooting."** Steve Jobs is cited as indicating that half the battle in being successful is simply perseverance.

PREPARATION: "When the Wind Blows"

The story is told of a farmer's helper who was newly hired despite his puzzling comment that his greatest strength was that he **"can sleep when the wind blows."** Not long after, a severe storm blew in, and when the farmer went to get this lad's help, he found him soundly asleep. Awakened, he stated, "I can sleep when the wind blows." In the morning, when the storm had passed, the farmer found that all his animals and property had been secured without suffering any damage, as the helper had prepared for the storm so that he could "sleep when the wind blows."

American Boy Scouts have as their motto, "Be Prepared." The U.S. Coast Guard has essentially this as their motto, too, in Latin: *Semper Paratus*, "always prepared." For most activities a great way to insure you are prepared is to have a check-list, just as airplane pilots and astronauts use to prevent overlooking anything important. Benjamin Franklin is quoted, "By failing to prepare you are preparing to fail."

COMMUNICATION: A Lost Art

Dr. Shufeldt quotes playwright and essayist George Bernard Shaw, "The single biggest problem in communication is the illusion that it has taken place."

To communicate successfully, we need to check and re-check that our audience has heard and understood our message. In college I was told that in giving a speech, you should "tell them what you are going to say, then say it, then tell them what you have said."

Speak and write simply where possible.

Don't cross your arms or clench your fists, nor roll your eyes in response when spoken to. Maintain eye contact. Don't speak and run, commenting as you fly by. Use proper grammar and spelling. Avoid empty sounds, like "uh" and "you know."

If someone stops listening to you, stop talking. When others talk, listen carefully, as listening well is a key to understanding and successful communicating.

IMPERTURBABILITY: Staying Calm

In his poem *If*, Rudyard Kipling advises, "keep your head when all about you are losing theirs and blaming it on you…trust yourself when all men doubt you…." In a crisis, calm is key; one must make haste slowly. One does not want to be like Chicken Little, who thought the sky was falling and ran around alarming the other farm animals. Dr. Shufeldt quotes the late Reverend Norman Vincent Peale (1952): "The cyclone derives its powers from a calm center. So does a person."

TOLERATING RISK: Being a Doer, not a Dreamer

Dr. Shufeldt emphasizes that entrepreneurism is risky, quoting the joke that "the way to make a small fortune in business is to start with a large fortune."

Sure, most new businesses go broke, but some succeed and some make it big, which may appeal to you. Shufeldt has been involved with successes and failures and knows "try, try again" has got to be balanced against "don't beat a dead horse." As the song goes, "know when to hold 'em, know when to fold 'em." There is a life cycle in new businesses: innovator, imitator, idiot.

If you want to run a business, let me recommend you read Kevin D. Johnson's (2013) *The Entrepreneur Mind,* with his discussion of 100 characteristics of the successful entrepreneur. You have to be a visualizer and an actualizer.

KINDNESS: The Art of Paying it Forward

Dr. Shufeldt gives several examples of lives changed by simple acts of kindness, including that of Frederick Douglass who became outstanding writer, publisher, and orator despite being born into slavery. We are urged to go beyond WIIFM [What's In It For Me]. Dr. Shufeldt maintains that his own acts of charity have in fact ended up benefiting him even more. Mark Twain is quoted, "Kindness is a language which the deaf can hear and the blind can read."

LEARNING: A Lifetime Pursuit

Continuing to learn is essential. Socrates is quoted as saying, "A wise man knows he knows nothing." Late in his long life, Michelangelo wrote on one of his sketches, *Ancora imparo,* "I am still learning." The late, great Nobel-Prize-winning physicist, Richard P. Feynman called himself a "curious character," continually wondering "why?"

Shufeldt urges us to read, read, read, and take classes. I enjoyed his quote from Winston Churchill, "I began my education at a very early age—in fact, right after I left college." **The self-taught American writer Eric Hoffer [read his (Hoffer, 1966) *The True***

Believer, if you get a chance], wrote, "The future belongs to the learners—not the knowers."

OPTIMISM/ENTHUSIASM: Look on the Bright Side

Shufeldt claims to be optimistic, almost to a fault, but writes that it allows him to view difficulties as opportunities. **Blind optimism would be wrong, but a rationally positive view helps keep us going.**

The story is told about writer and editor Norman Cousins, who overcame cancer largely through his unwillingness to acknowledge defeat and, instead, his focus on humor and laughter. Many other examples are presented, including that of the Reverend Norman Vincent Peale (1952), author of the best-selling guide, *The Power of Positive Thinking,* who distinguished between the "energetic optimists" and the "purveyors of gloom." Dr. Peale founded *Guideposts,* an inspiring monthly magazine with a circulation of over two million.

Shufeldt writes, "enthusiasm is infectious—spread it." Science fiction novelist Robert A Heinlein, one of my favorites, notes that even if pessimists were right more often than optimists, being optimistic is more fun.

PERSPECTIVE: Changing It Changes Everything

It has been said, "Where you stand depends on where you sit." Our cherished positions are often determined by our "points of view," our perspectives. Dr. Shufeldt maintains that the most important lesson life has taught him is that life is about perspective: changing your perspective changes everything.

Southwest Airlines' phenomenal success is accredited largely to their philosophy of putting their employees first, on the theory that happy employees will treat customers right. One guru has advised, "You choose to worry or you choose not to." Another enjoins us to focus on the journey, not the destination. **My favorite quote on the topic is, from Horace Walpole, "Life is a comedy to those that think, a tragedy to those that feel."**

INDEFATIGABLE: Empty the Tank!

When you are engaged in something worth doing, do it all the way. Go the extra mile. Use up all the gasoline in your tank. We can do more than we think we can. Run your marathon flat out. Go all in, beyond your comfort zone.

Shufeldt cites one of his favorite movies and mine, *Chariots of Fire,* which starts with beautiful footage of British runners in training, doing their utmost. He reminds us of the brave passengers on United Flight 93 on September 11, 2001, who, led by Todd Beamer and inspired by his "Let's roll," overcame the hijackers intent on crashing the plane into one of the government buildings in Washington, DC. They indeed gave their all.

As Kipling wrote, we are to "fill the unforgiving minute with sixty seconds' worth of distance run."

Digresssion: "Do you like Kipling," he asked.
"I don't know," she replied. "I've never kippled."

EFFICIENCY: Doing Better What's Being Done

Theodore Roosevelt lived only 59 years, yet achieved amazing feats, as a warrior, explorer, statesman, writer, the youngest man inaugurated as President, and he served two terms. He lived life to the fullest and did so efficiently.

Management expert Peter Drucker is cited, **"Efficiency is doing things right; effectiveness is doing the right things."** Both are important. Shufeldt advises us to have goals that we put into writing: "S.M.A.R.T. goals, goals which are Specific, Measurable, Achievable, Realistic, and Time-bound." Then we must act on them.

Have a "to-do" list and work on it. Your daily list should likely have only a few, most important, elements. The founder of Amazon, Jeff Bezos, is credited with having found a new way to conduct a retail business. Bezos emphasizes that Amazon is "customer-centric." That's being effective.

INTEGRITY: A Priceless Commodity

"Simply put, integrity is doing what you say and saying what you'll do," Shufeldt writes. "Integrity" is derived from the Latin word for wholeness. Cheating is anathema to those with integrity. Examples of integrity in sports, such as golf, where players have cost themselves victories by calling fouls on themselves, are given.

Former U.S. Senator from Wyoming Alan K. Simpson stated, "If you have integrity, nothing else matters. If you don't have integrity, nothing else matters."

INTUITION: Your Guts Don't Lie

While the preceding discussion has emphasized accentuating the positive, there are times when fear is appropriate, and you must "listen to your gut." Our "fight or flight" response may be needed and we must avoid "freeze." Whether you are walking in a strange area at night or surfing an unfamiliar site on the Internet, you need to be cautious.

Shufeldt notes there is an organization named "Heartless Bitches International" that has a web site listing hundreds of "red flags" people should heed in developing relationships. Sexy actress of the last century, Mae West, is quoted, "Don't marry a man to reform him. That's what reform schools are for." Google uses a "red flag" for myriad sites with warnings. Lies are red flags, as are rudeness, arrogance, laziness, negativity, tough pre-hire ne-gotiation, callousness, excuses, misspellings.... Shufeldt warns, "In my experience, women have better gut instincts than men, but are less likely to follow them."

Finally, Dr. Shufeldt advises:

THE RARE FIND: Become the One of a Kind

Actress Bernadette Peters is quoted: "You've gotta be original, because if you're like someone else, what do they need you for?" Don't try to be just any kind of unique, but uniquely good. American essayist Ralph Waldo Emerson, a favorite of mine, wrote, "Trust thyself: every heart vibrates to that iron string." It's lonely at the top, sometimes, but the air is clean and the view is terrific.

Dr. Shufeldt acknowledges that much of this we have heard before, but it is worth repeating. In just under 200 pages, he includes his own observations and anecdotes along with those of many other successful people and students of success. The work is a virtual handbook for those who hope to be outstanding, like you.

RESOURCES

*Knowledge is of two kinds: we know a subject ourselves or
we know where we can find information on it.*
Samuel Johnson

INTERNET, LIBRARIES, SOCIETIES, ENCYCLOPEDIAS, THESAURUS, DICTIONARY

In the blog by Carol Tice, makealivingwriting.com, guest writer Samantha Drake gave the following source tips so "writers can find facts fast—and make sure they're true":

- **Governments:** For the U.S. see Centers for Disease Control and the National Institutes of Health, USA.gov, Data.gov, and Government Information Online, which lets you mail questions to librarians. The individual states have many agencies willing to provide reliable data.
- **Major national organizations:** Such as the American Cancer Society, the Ewing Marion Kauffman Foundation, the American Institute of Certified Professional Accountants, *etc.*
- **Trade organizations:** Her example of such a publication was *Nation's Restaurant News*.

- **Name-brand studies and surveys:** Examples given were Pew Research Center and Gallup.
- **Beware:** Wikipedia can be a useful start, but is not authoritative. Use its references yourself to trace the item to its source. "Studies" by organizations with strong views are also to be treated with suspicion.

A truly mammoth source of information on self-publishing is appropriately titled *The Complete Guide to Self-publishing: Everything You Need to Know to Write, Publish, Promote, and Sell Your Own Book*. The fifth edition is copyrighted in 2010 by its authors Marilyn Ross and Susan Collier. It is published by Writers Digest Books, Cincinnati Ohio. These authors suggest you also visit the website writersdigest.com/books.

An abridged version of their Table of Contents follows:

Part I. TODAY'S PUBLISHING SCENE

- Your Portal to Self-Publishing: Enter Here
- Alternatives for Getting Into Print: From POD to Subsidy Publishing—and Everything In Between
- Cyberoptions—Reading between the Lines of Ebooks

PART II: START-UP

- Scoping Out a Marketable Subject
- Product Development: Writing Your Own Book or Booklet
- Establishing Your Publishing Company and Generating Capital

- Mastering Operating Procedures
- Must-Do Important Early Activities

PART III: CREATING A QUALITY PRODUCT THAT ATTRACTS BUYERS

- Wow! Design and Typesetting
- Affordable Book Manufacturing—the Printing Process

PART IV: KILLER PR—THE GREAT EQUALIZER

- Initiating a Nationwide Marketing Plan with Publicity Pizzazz
- Using the Web to Rally "Buzz" and Business
- Provocative Promotional Strategies
- Turning Book Signings into Stellar Events

PART V: SELLING BOOKS THE USUAL WAYS

- Milking the Standard Channels of Distribution
- Creating Ads that Reel in Results
- Direct Marketing Smarts
- Tapping into Lucrative Subsidiary Rights

PART VI: NONTRADITIONAL VENUES FOR GENERATING MORE SALES

- Social Media
- Originating Extraordinary "Out-of-the-Box" Opportunities
- Seminars, Classes, and Trade Shows Can Multiply Your Profits

PART VII: PROPELLING YOUR BUSINESS THROUGH THE STRATOSPHERE

- Bagging the Big Game: Selling Your Self-Published Book to a Goliath
- Enlarge Your Kingdom; Move up to "Small Press" Status

This approximately 200,000-word guide goes far beyond what we can cover here. It is available through Amazon for $17 for the paperback and $11 for the Kindle ebook version, the one I bought for myself.

Another excellent resource for new authors is the book by J. Steve Miller and Cherie K. Miller, *Sell More Books! Book Marketing and Publishing for Low-Profile and Debut Authors: Rethinking Book Publicity after the Digital Revolution.* Wisdom Creek Press, LLC. 2011.

Their Table of Contents is as follows:

Part I
Rethink Book Marketing in Light of the Revolutions

Chapter 1: Four Digital Revolutions that Can Make Nobodies Awesome

Part II
From Nobody to Somebody
Build Platforms with a Marketable Book and a
Cool Online Presence

Chapter 2: Why Market Your Book?

Appendix 2: 200+ Ways that Low-Profile Authors Can Market
Their Books
Endnotes

Clearly, this 344-page compendium of useful book marketing information in this new age of publishing is a bargain at $10 for the paperback and $4 for the Kindle ebook through amazon. com.

Get Slightly Famous: Become a Celebrity in Your Field and Attract More Business with Less Effort by Steven Van Yoder (2012) tells how to become known among your potential customers, and is very favorably reviewed at amazon.com, where it is available for $10 as a Kindle ebook and $18 for the paperback version.

Book Yourself Solid: The Fastest, Easiest, and Most Reliable System for Getting More Clients Than You Can Handle Even If You Hate Marketing and Selling, by Michael Port (2010), is also widely heralded at amazon.com, where it is available as a Kindle ebook for $10 and as a paperback for $11. Techniques for those selling their services are readily adaptable to those selling their books. Many who sell books hope to use them to increase demand for their services, linking the two.

Finally, don't forget those old standbys: encyclopedias, a thesaurus, and a dictionary.

ABOUT THE AUTHOR

Douglas Winslow Cooper is a writer and retired environmental physicist, now helping to manage at-home nursing care of his wife. Cooper earned his A.B., with honors, in physics at Cornell, then served at the U.S. Army biological warfare laboratories at Ft. Detrick, MD. Subsequently, he returned to school, obtaining his M.S. degree in physics at Penn State and his Ph.D. in engineering from Harvard. His professional life centered on environmental issues. He was the author or co-author of more than 100 technical articles published in refereed journals and was elected Fellow of the Institute of Environmental Sciences. In 2011 he wrote and published *Ting and I: A Memoir of Love, Courage, and Devotion,* available at amazon.com and other online booksellers. Dr. Cooper does freelance writing, book partnering and editing. He co-authored a detective's memoir, *The Shield of Gold,* and another memoir, *Kidnapped Twice;* he co-authored *SOLVED! Curing Your Medical Insurance Problems,* and he edited the memoirs *High Shoes and Bloomers, But…at What Cost,* and *Home Is Where the Story Begins.* His web sites are:

http://douglaswinslowcooper.blogspot.com
http://writeyourbookwithme.com
http://tingandi.com
http://managenursingcareathome.com

EDUCATION

Ph.D., Engineering, Harvard University, 1974.

M.S., Physics, The Pennsylvania State University, 1969.

A.B., Physics, Cornell University, 1964.

POST-PH.D. EMPLOYMENT

Physicist, GCA / Technology Division, Bedford, MA. Conducted air pollution research, 1973-76.

Assistant Professor and then Associate Professor of Environmental Physics, Harvard School of Public Health, Boston, MA. Taught environmental management and aerosol science and assisted in teaching introductory biostatistics and a health policy course. Performed research related to air pollution, industrial hygiene, and nuclear reactor health effects modeling. Became Director, Environmental Health Management Program, 1976-83.

Research Staff Member, IBM T.J. Watson Research Center, Yorktown Heights, NY. Carried out research and did internal consulting and training on topics related to contamination control, measurement, and analysis, often involving statistical analysis and mathematical modeling, 1983-93.

Director, Contamination Control, The Texwipe Company, Upper Saddle River, NJ. Performed research and wrote technical articles on contamination control to improve its products and support the company's technical reputation. Managed contamination-related quality control, 1993-2000. Then, retired.

COME, WRITE YOUR BOOK WITH ME

If you want to participate in these 5 Ps—Plan, Prepare, Publish, Promote, and Payoff—I would be happy to partner with you, as coach, editor, possibly co-author. Contact me at http://www. writeyourbookwithme.com or at douglas@tingandi.com.

Our first session will be free; we will explore your writing goals and discuss how you can achieve them.

REVIEW?

If you would be kind enough to review this book, say at amazon.com or Goodreads, it would help potential readers as well as the author.

REFERENCES

There are several style systems for citations in the text and for noting references at the end, including those of the Modern Language Association (MLA) and the American Psychological Association (APA). Here I use APA, as well as I can. A fine source is the ebook by Kristin G. Hatch, *APA Format 101* (Hatch, 2014). Here's her example for a book reference:

Hill, N. (1983). *Think and grow rich.* NY: Fawcett Crest.

I can use this just as it is, since I cited his book (Hill, 1983) in my text.

For two authors, such as (Palloff & Pratt, 2007), whom I do not cite, the reference would be:

Palloff, M.R., & Pratt, K. (2007). *Building online communities.* San Francisco, CA: John Wiley & Sons, Inc.

For three to seven authors, "List all authors on the reference page, and when you first make your first in-text citation. After that you can use *et al*....."

I read most of my references as Kindle ebooks from Amazon.

Where this is noted, it does not mean that Amazon is the sole source nor that the book is only available in ebook format, just that it is available that way.

Adams, R.L. (2013). *Viral: How to spread your ideas like a virus.* Amazon ebook.

Adkins, S. (2015). *Squashing liberalism.* In preparation.

Allen, M. (2014). *Sell more books: self-publisher's guide to getting a top selling book.* Amazon ebook.

Axtell, J. (2014). *But…at what cost.* Denver, CO: Outskirts Press.

Bareham, S. (2012). *eBook author success guide—1: Self-publishing eBooks.* Nelson, B.C., Canada: Summa Publishing.

Barrington, J. (2002). *Writing a memoir.* Portland, OR: The Eighth Mountain Press.

Barry, S., & Goldmark, K.K., (2010). *Write that book already! The tough love you need to get published now.* Avon, MA: Adams Media.

Bauby, J.-D. (1997).*The diving bell and the butterfly.* New York: Random House.

Bolt, C., & Roper, J. (2015) *Book launch: how to write, market, and self-publish your first bestseller in 3 months or less AND use it to start & grow a six-figure business.* Amazon ebook.

Brooks, R., & Richardson, B.L. (2012). *You should really write a book: How to write, sell and market your memoir.* London: St. Martin's Griffin. Amazon ebook.

Card, O.S. (2001). *How to write science fiction and fantasy.* Amazon ebook. Ft. Collins, CO: Writer's Digest Books.

Carnegie, D. (1937, 2010). *How to win friends and influence people.* New York: Simon & Schuster. Amazon ebook.

Carter, G. (2015). *The business book outline builder.* England: Marketing Twenty-One, LTD. Amazon ebook.

Cooper, D.W. (2011) *Ting and I: A memoir of love, courage, and devotion.* Denver, CO: Outskirts Press.

Cooper, D.W., and Beggin, D.R., (2016) *How to manage nursing care at home.* In preparation. Denver, CO: Outskirts Press.

Cooper, D.W., & Foglia, M.E. (2012). *Ava Gardner's daughter? An investigation into two women's pasts.* Denver, CO: Outskirts Press.

Covey, S.R. (1989, 2007) *The 7 habits of highly effective people.* La Jolla, CA: Simon & Schuster.

Eckstein, K. (2013). *AUTHOR'S QUICK GUIDE to creating a killer non-fiction book title.* High Point, NC: Discover! Books. Amazon ebook.

Evans, S. (2015). *Novel writing mastery: proven and simple techniques to outline, structure and write a successful novel.* Amazon ebook.

Frankl, V. (2006). *Man's search for meaning.* Boston, MA: Beacon Press.

Freedman, D. F. (2010). *Wrong: Why experts keep failing us— and how to know when not to trust them.* New York, NY: Little, Brown. Amazon ebook.

Garcia, H.F. (2012). *The power of communication: Skills to build trust, inspire loyalty, and lead effectively.* Upper Saddle River, NJ: FT Press. Amazon ebook.

Gibran, K. (1973). *The prophet.* New York: A.A. Knopf.

Gladwell, M. (2006). *The tipping point.* New York: Hachette Book Group.

Golino, L., & Cooper, D.W. (2013), *The shield of gold: A candid memoir by a NYPD detective.* Denver, CO: Outskirts Press. Amazon ebook.

Grahl, T. (2013). *Your first 1000 copies: The step-by-step guide to marketing your book.* Out:think. Amazon ebook.

Gray, J. (1992). *Men are from Mars, women are from Venus.* New York: Harper Collins paperback and ebook.

Gross, A.G., & Cooper, D.W. (2015) *SOLVED! curing your medical insurance problems.* Denver, CO: Outskirts Press.

Hall, R. (2015). *Why does my book not sell? 20 simple fixes.* St Leonards, UK: Scimitar Press.

Hanley-Goff, M.J. (2014). *Writing can get you through the tough times: No experience necessary.* Bloomington, IN: Balboa Press. Paperback and Amazon ebook.

Hatch, K.G. (2014). *APA format 101: The simplified guide.* Amazon ebook.

Hazard, M. (2015). *Corus and the case of the chaos: A detective mystery.* Amazon ebook.

Hill, N. (1983). *Think and grow rich.* NY: Fawcett Crest.

Hillman, R. (2015). *17 reasons why you should write a book.* Amazon ebook.

Hitz, S. (2014) *How to write a book from outline to finish line.* Amazon ebook.

Hoffer, E. (1986). *The true believer.* New York: Perennial Library. Also Harper Collins ebook.

Ingermanson, R., & Economy, P. (2009). *Writing fiction for dummies.* Hoboken, NJ: Wiley Publishing.

Jacob, D. (2015) *Will write for food: the complete guide to writing cookbooks, blogs, reviews, memoirs, and more.* Philadelphia: Da Capo Press. Amazon ebook.

Johnson, K.D. (2013). *The entrepreneur mind: 100 essential beliefs, characteristics, and habits of elite entrepreneurs.* Atlanta, GA: Johnson Media Inc. Amazon ebook.

Karia, A. (2015). *How to write a non-fiction Kindle ebook in 15 days,* Self-Published. Amazon ebook.

King, S. (2000). *On writing: a memoir of the craft.* New York: Scribner.

Kiyosaki, R.T. (2000). *Rich dad, poor dad: What the rich teach their kids about money—that the poor and middle-class do not.* New York: Warner Business Books.

J.P. Kurzitza (2011). *So you want to write a novel.* Edmonton, Alberta, Canada: Purple Punk Publishing. Amazon ebook.

Locke, J. (2011). *How I sold 1 million ebooks in 5 months.* Long Boat Key, FL: Telemachus Press. Amazon ebook.

Merton, T. (1948, 1978). *The seven-storey mountain.* New York: Harcourt Brace.

Michaels, L. (2007). *On writing romance: how to craft a novel that sells.* Ft. Collins, CO: Writer's Digest Books. Amazon ebook.

Miller, J.S., & Miller, C.K. (2011) *Sell more books! Book marketing and publishing for low-profile and debut authors: Rethinking book publicity after the digital revolution.* Acworth, GA: Wisdom Creek Press, LLC. Amazon ebook.

Olson, J.S. (2009). *The unselfish guide to self-promotion: How to promote yourself, your ideas and your products.* Cube 17, Inc. Amazon ebook.

Peale, N.V. (1952). *The power of positive thinking.* Upper Saddle River, NJ: Prentice Hall.

Penn, J. (2015). *How to make a living with your writing: books, blogging and more.* The Creative Penn Limited. Amazon ebook.

Pickens, L.Q. (2016). *The last drumbeat. In preparation.*

Port, M. (2010) *Book yourself solid: The fastest, easiest, and most reliable system for getting more clients than you can handle even if you hate marketing and selling,* Amazon ebook.

Poynter, D. (2000). Books*: Tips, stories, & advice on writing, publishing and promoting.* Santa Barbara, CA: Para Publishing. Amazon ebook.

Ross, M., & Collier, S. (2010). *The complete guide to self-publishing: Everything you need to know to write, publish, promote, and sell your own book.* Cincinnati, OH: Writers Digest Books.

Shufeldt, J. (2013). *The ingredients of outliers: A recipe for personal achievement.* Scottsdale, AZ: Outliers Publishing. Amazon ebook.

Seaman, M.E., & Cooper, D.W. (2015). *Kidnapped twice: Then betrayed and abused.* Denver, CO: Outskirts Press. Amazon ebook.

Selfridge, A.C. (2014). *High shoes and bloomers.* Denver, CO: Outskirts Press.

Shields, K.L. (2015). *Home is where the story begins: Memoir of a happy childhood.* Denver, CO: Outskirts Press.

Stanley, T.J. (2010), *The millionaire next door. New York:* Rosetta Books.

Strunk, W., Jr., & White, E.B. (1999). *The elements of style.* New York: Longman.

Sumsion, S. (2010). *Produce, publish, publicize.* Dwight, NE: Sanguine Publishing. Amazon ebook.

Taleb, N.N. (2012). *Antifragile: Things that gain from disorder.* New York: Random House.

Twead, V. (2015). *How to write a bestselling memoir: Three steps to success.* Ant Press. Amazon ebook.

Waters, D. & Waters, L. (1997). *Speak and grow rich.* Upper Saddle River, NJ: Prentice Hall. Paperback and Amazon ebook.

Van Yoder (2012) *Get slightly famous: Become a celebrity in your field and attract more business with less effort.* Printed by CreateSpace. Amazon ebook.

APPENDIX I.
ACTIVITY AND PROGRESS RECORD

WEEK ONE

Saturday, outlined.	w/c= 500.	Added 500.
Sunday, wrote up to WHY WRITE.	w/c= 2,500.	Added 2,000.
Sunday, added prior blogs.	w/c=17,900.	Added 15,400.
Sunday, more writing,	w/c=20,100.	Added 2,200.
Monday, more writing,	w/c=21,840.	Added 1,740.
Tuesday, more writing,	w/c=24,800	Added 2,960
Tuesday, deleted 1000 duplicates,	w/c=23,870	Added 0
Wednesday, organized, planned, wrote,	w/c=26,030	Added 2,160.
Thursday, wrote,	w/c=26,880	Added 850.
Friday, wrote nothing, added file,	w/c= 27,350	Added 470.

WEEK TWO

Saturday, wrote, revised to p.72	w/c= 28,700	Added 1,350
Sunday, wrote, revised to p.82	w/c= 29,300	Added 600
Monday, wrote 0, revised 0	w/c= 29,300	Added 0
Tuesday, wrote, revised to p.119	w/c= 29,840	Added 540
Wednesday, 2nd revision to p.57	w/c= 30,260	Added 420
Thursday, added Hall (2015) matter	w/c = 31,730	Added 1470
Friday, proofread a different book.	w/c = 31,730	Added 0

WEEK THREE

Saturday, wrote, added references	w/c= 32,470	Added 740
Sunday, wrote, added references	w/c= 33,000	Added 530
Monday, wrote, added reference	w/c= 33,340	Added 340
Tuesday, wrote, added references	w/c= 33,560	Added 220
Wednesday, wrote, added reference	w/c= 34,270	Added 710
Thursday, wrote, added reference	w/c = 35,080	Added 810
Friday, wrote, added references	w/c = 35,510	Added 430

WEEK FOUR

Saturday, wrote, formatted, proofed	w/c = 35,810	Added 300
Sunday, wrote, formatted, proofed	w/c = 36,170	Added 360
Monday, formatted, proofed	w/c = 36,240	Added 70
Tuesday, add Barry & Goldmark (2010)	w/c = 36,540	Added 300
Wednesday, References + Grahl (2013)	w/c = 37,200	Added 660
Thursday, add Carter on ghostwriting	w/c = 38,190	Added 990
Friday, proofed, reordered	w/c = 38,230	Added 40

WEEK FIVE

Saturday, added …Make a Living…	w/c = 38,950	Added 720
Sunday, added …Sell More Books…	w/c = 39,400	Added 450
Monday, added stuff but forgot to note it or I lost it on computer.		
Tuesday, added more	w/c = 40,630	Added 1,230
Wednesday, added more	w/c = 41,050	Added 420
Thursday, quotations for chapter heads	w/c = 41,170	Added 120
Friday, list references on notepad	w/c = 41,180	Added 10

WEEK SIX

Saturday, alphabetized refs, add info	w/c = 41,330	Added 150
Sunday, worked on refs,	w/c = 41,460	Added 130
Monday, worked on refs,	w/c = 41,640	Added 180
Tuesday, worked on refs,	w/c = ?	

Wednesday, finished refs.	w/c = 42,040	Added 400
Thursday, sum Evans (2015).	w/c = 42,480	Added 440
Friday, citations / refs.	w/c = 42,520	Added 40

WEEK SEVEN

Saturday, revised up to Strunk.	w/c = 42,620	Added 100
Sunday, revised up to Compelling Intro.	w/c = 42,690	Added 70
Monday, revised up to history	w/c = 42,740	Added 50
Tuesday, revised up to romance	w/c = 42,850	Added 110
Wednesday, revised to GOING VIRAL	w/c = 42,910	Added 60
Thursday, revised to Bolt, p.121	w/c = 42,920	Added 10
Friday, revised to Reflections	w/c = 42,940	Added 20

WEEK EIGHT

Saturday, revised to "Penultimate Draft"   w/c = 42,960   Added 20
[Sunday, bought Outskirts Sapphire pkg for WYBWM 154929E. -$400]
Sunday, did "Tell Their Stories" for Asiance, blogged; checked TOC
Monday, Blog: Wholesaler's sum (3498 chars + spaces, 540 words)
Tuesday, DWC PHD LLC spreadsheet created.
Wednesday, collect email addresses of cited authors. Saw webinar.
Thursday, sent few cited authors Word ms. Wrote. w/c 43,200 173pp
Friday, correspondence and proofing.

WEEK NINE

Saturday, proofing.
Sunday, correct file. Wrote re: covers, price. w/c 43,550   Added 350
Monday, files to copy center for copies.
Tuesday, got copies back. Answered "Fair Use" query from publisher.
Wednesday, Really Penultimate Draft to proofreaders.
Thursday, no progress.
Friday, responded to Steve Miller email.

WEEK TEN

Saturday, corrections to Multi-Payer Medicine Nightmare

Sunday, no progress.

Monday, add C. Cohen corrections and Acknowledgment.

Tuesday, more on Multi-Payer Medicine Nightmare corrections.

Wednesday, sent Really Penultimate Draft to about 50 friends.

Thursday, added "Praise for…" section: Guzman, Miller, Nolly

Friday, no progress.

WEEK ELEVEN

Saturday, went to seminar, added Hanley-Goff (2014). w/c 44,220.

Sunday, no activity. Awaiting responses from emailing.

Monday, lunched with author K.B. Shields. Author correspondence.

Tuesday, worked on HTMNCAH book.

Wednesday, met with advisor, listed 36 video promo topics.

Thursday, 3 September 2015. Beloved sister, Diana, died last night.

WEEK TWELVE

Saturday, funeral.

Sunday, corresponded with Ginny Carter, the Author Maker.

Monday through Friday, nothing.

WEEK THIRTEEN

Saturday, Sunday, nothing.

Monday, added Ginny Carter blurb. Sent final to Outskirts Press.

CPSIA information can be obtained at www.ICGtesting.com
Printed in the USA
BVOW02s0524110116

432403BV00002B/186/P

9 781478 764281